Dept of Art Community
Christmas 1964

Fr. Luke Fester ofm

Saint Madeleine Sophie Barat

Saint Madeleine Sophie Barat

Mother C. E. MAGUIRE, R.S.C.J

SHEED AND WARD – *NEW YORK*

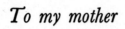

To my mother

Contents

Contents

Saint Madeleine Sophie Barat

Introduction

Saints' lives (unless the biographer is dull) make good stories. At any rate, Aristotle should have thought so, for saints have all the qualities he demanded in successful characters. He wanted them, in tragedies at least, to be "better than most men," true to type, true to life, and—most of all—consistent. Saints are obviously better than most men. Whether or not you think them true to type and to life depends on what you know of types and of life. But there is no doubt whatever that they are consistent along one line. At some point in their career, early or late, they come to know a man who lived when the Roman Empire was beginning and who so impressed his contemporaries and eventually half the rest of the world that we date the happenings of history by whether they came before or after Him. Having come to "know" this man, the saints have also been convinced that He is God. If you really believe there is a God who made you, who became man and lived the life of man and left behind instructions about how other men were to live, then—if you are consistent—you should be a saint. Very few people seem, of course, to be saints. Even those who honestly believe what the saints believe work only in fits and starts at following the instructions, for the instructions are not easy to follow. They enter into the most annoyingly personal details of a man's life, and allow no vacations. So most people who call themselves Christians—and *are* Christians because they believe Christ was and is God—obey His orders only more or less, as it suits their convenience. But saints are consistent. They follow orders all the time, all the way; and when there is no specific order to follow, they do what they think Christ would have wanted them to do under the circumstances. And they like this way of acting; not because they are too lazy to think for themselves, or too scared to want anything except security, but because they have fallen in love with Christ.

This is the story of Madeleine Sophie Barat, a woman who lived to be very old, and in her eighty-five years was personally affected by three revolutions. She was born in a small town where her family was unknown by everyone who was anyone. She died in Paris, known and revered, far more than she wanted or liked to be, in social circles to which almost everyone else would have been delighted to belong. This was not her personal choice. She would have liked to spend her life either praying quietly in some Carmelite cloister or teaching very young, and preferably very poor, children. Instead she founded and governed a religious congregation which, in most of Europe and in North and South America, conducted schools for young ladies of means and position. To the end, she insisted upon reminding people of her humble origin, not by any inverted snobbery, or to show how far she had come, but to emphasize that she was herself of no importance whatever, that what had been done through her had been done by God working with most unpromising material, and that, if she achieved anything (which she doubted) it could not be estimated in terms of titles and money.

Her nuns taught girls who had titles and money, but that was because noble and wealthy girls had souls, and someone had to teach them if they were to be saved; and because that was evidently what God wanted. She herself taught and practised the strictest poverty and humility, and saw to it that a school for poor children was, if possible, carried on in every one of her convents. But the truth is that, to her, poor and rich, humble and noble, were irrelevant terms. A recent writer calls schools like hers places where women receive "early training in the ways of their world." This is true as far as it goes, but it ignores the reason why they must be so trained. Nuns think they must be trained whether they are rich or poor if they are to pass through the things of this life in such a way that they may not lose those which are eternal. Not that the things of this life should be underrated or condemned. They are important and sometimes pleasant, but they should be regarded as means to an end.

The end could most aptly be expressed as living happily ever after. The expression is especially apt because Madame Barat saw life as a love story. She had herself fallen in love with the man Christ who was God, because she knew God had become a man to convince men He loved them. She was convinced, and was willing—eager, even—to do whatever was required to demonstrate to God and to everyone else that she was convinced: to God because she wanted to receive the love He offered; to others so that they might receive it too. All who met her, from coach drivers to countesses, saw at once that she had received the love of God, and came to want it themselves. Many, because of her, did receive it. Many still do. The purpose of this book is to widen her acquaintance, so that now, almost a hundred years after her death, people may go on seeing what the love of God did in her and can do in them.

CHAPTER ONE

1779–1800

Joigny to Paris

Burgundy, like most of France, has a long tradition of those consistent Christians we call saints. Situated at the junction of northern and southern France, of what is grave and methodical in the culture of the North, and what is gay and graceful in that of the South of Europe, it has produced more orators and scholars than poets or novelists, more sculptors than painters. The typical Burgundian is not a man of imagination, much less fantasy. Yet in the middle ages, Burgundy was the most civilized part of France. There monasticism, which fed the culture of the West, had its heart and center. There were Cluny, Clairvaux, Citeaux. St. Bernard, on the side of a hill at Vézelay, preached the Second Crusade. He was the saint who did more than anyone except Francis of Assisi to turn medieval devotion to personal love of the God-Man; and Vézelay was the town with so much devotion to Mary Magdalen that the townsmen either stole or bribed from a church in Provence what were believed to be the relics of that great lover of Christ.

But both Bernard, who was one of their own, and Mary

Magdalen, whom they tried to naturalize, were practical lovers, whose practicality would appeal to hard-headed Burgundians. Bernard dotted all of Europe with monasteries where men proved their love, as he had proved his, by lives of severest austerity; and Mary Magdalen, according to the legend, had repaired the misplaced loves of her youth by years of penance even more severe. The same combination of love and practicality made Jane Frances de Chantal, from Dijon, the capital of Burgundy, found the Order of the Visitation, in which Margaret Mary Alacoque, a Burgundian peasant girl, was to receive the revelations of the Sacred Heart. Paray-le-Monial, where the revelations took place, is in Burgundy, too.

It was Joigny, a town in the northwestern corner of Burgundy, less than fifty miles from Vézelay, which produced a namesake of Mary Magdalen, Madeleine Sophie Barat, who carried on the work of Margaret Mary Alacoque, and found her best and dearest helper in Philippine Duchesne, a daughter of Jane Frances de Chantal. The pattern has Burgundian neatness.

Joigny is a medieval town, with the usual local combination of charm and severity. It is set on the side of a hill up the slope of which the houses climb to a castle at the top. The streets are narrow and steep, but the town has its own beauty. At the foot of the hill wind the slow, clear waters of the river Yonne between lush meadows and poplar groves.

The family of Jacques Barat lived in a street called Puits-Chardon (now Rue Davier) in a house with three floors. On the night of December 12, in 1779, a fire broke out in a house nearby, and so frightened Jacques Barat's wife that her third child was born two months ahead of time. As was appropriate in a town so near to Vézelay, all the Barat women were called Madeleine. The mother was Marie-Madeleine (her maiden name was Fouffé) and the elder sister Marie Louise Madeleine. The new daughter also became Madeleine, with Sophie added, when she was baptized hastily next day. Her godfather, in the ceremony under the high vaults and richly colored windows of the church of St. Thibault, was her brother, Louis, eleven years older than herself.

Jacques Barat earned a good steady living. He owned some vineyards on the slopes outside the town, and he made and sold the barrels so much in demand in a wine-growing section. He was not, by all reports, a fast thinking man, but he did not need to be, and he had more valuable qualities: he was hard working and reliable, and had the respect and liking of his neighbors; he was patient, and perhaps seemed more so in contrast with his wife. Madeleine Fouffé, better educated than her husband, and probably more intelligent, was also more ambitious for her children and more inclined to live on her emotions.

There was every chance that Sophie, as she was called to distinguish her in the trio of Madeleines, would be spoiled. She had almost cost Madeleine Fouffé her life, she was younger than any of the other children, and she was very frail. Besides, she had inherited both her mother's intelligence and liveliness and her father's common sense and knack for getting along with people. Anecdotes which may have been prompted by hindsight insist upon her wit, her precociously good judgment, her gift for seeing through complicated situations and making them sound simple to others. But she was no prig. She loved games and played them well, and she had her mother's strong affections. Her affections were, in fact, so strong and so vividly expressed that they worried her brother Louis, who intended to be a priest. As her godfather, he kept a watchful eye on her during his holidays from the school at Joigny, and later as a student and then a teacher at the seminary of Sens.

All we know of Louis Barat indicates that he had almost all the qualifications of a pious and holy priest, but that he had little sense of humor. He had received from his mother, and perhaps from his seminary training, a strongly rigoristic bias. There is no doubt that his sister was far more gifted than he. Being the more narrow of the two, he looked with suspicion at whatever in her he could not understand, and, with a godfather's privileges added to those of a priest-to-be, he took her in hand. His prescription to save her from her vivid imagination, her liveliness and what he thought her overstrong emotions was study, study in the awesome tradition of French schoolboys. As it turned out, it was not a bad prescription, though it was administered ruthlessly. Her superiority could have made her stubborn, petulant and caustic. To prevent this, Louis gave her more than enough to exercise her mind on, and systematically kept her from having her own way. Because he was young and inexperienced, he carried his severity too far, and it took years of later and milder direction to correct its bad effects. On the whole, it is surprising how little harm he did. What saved them both was that he was honestly fond of his little sister and had the highest respect for her gifts, and that she, because she returned his affection, did not resent his high-handed methods. This lack of resentment in her, her instinctive willingness to believe in people's good intentions, partly explains her lifelong power of winning friends.

She was barely seven years old when Louis began to put his well-thought-out educational system into practice. Beginning with Bible history and the history of France, he went on to grammar, arithmetic, physics and geometry. Besides learning Latin and Greek and memorizing long passages of Homer and Virgil, she was to be introduced to Italian and Spanish. Luckily, Louis was not always at home, and though he left assignments for her to do when he was away, she at first got out of them when she could. Her mother, torn between pride at what she was learning and fear that she was being worked too hard, approved of her few innocent escapades. But the terrible brother had a way of appearing at inconvenient moments, and Sophie, off in the vineyards playing with her friends, was hurriedly haled home to be scolded and put back to her books by her implacable brother, who, as his Jesuit biographer later wrote with evident approval, had never had any attraction for games in his youth, and who frowned on Sophie's honest attraction for what he called "bagatelles."

It is no wonder that so well-followed-up a scholar was far ahead of children of her age in catechism classes taught by the parish priest. But it was a century before small children were allowed to receive Holy Communion, and Sophie's pastor let her do so, as a great favor, only at the age of ten. The year was 1789.

The date may explain Louis Barat's somber outlook on life. From Joigny to Paris was less than a hundred miles, and Sens was even nearer the capital. A conscientious, intelligent cler-

ical student must have watched with anxiety the growth of unrest in the district. There had for a long time been a close link,
in France, between Church and State, with the State often dic-
tating the terms on which the Church might function. What
effect would possible changes have on Louis Barat's own career
and on the religious life of ordinary Frenchmen? He could
probably not have foreseen how far-reaching the changes
would be; but he must have known the anti-religious thinking
of certain circles. It was understandable, under the circumstances, that he should want to arm his gay and gifted young
sister against the future.

As it turned out, even he was not sufficiently armed against
it, though he drove himself harder than he drove her. Worse
for him than all the murder and castle-burning that began soon
enough, worse than the fear, and the fanning of political and
personal passions by newspapers and revolutionary clubs, was
the uncertainty of how priests should react to the new Civil
Constitution of the Clergy. Bishops had fought it. The Pope
had not been consulted about it. The King hesitated to sign it.
It confiscated church property, closed religious houses, arranged that bishops and priests should be elected by the public. Unless a priest took an oath to support it, he was not allowed
to fulfill his priestly functions. Louis Barat was only a deacon,
but since he taught in the Joigny school, he had to take the
oath. Why should he not? He had been brought up by a clergy
which accepted a certain amount of State control. After all, his
archbishop had taken the oath, and Loménie de Brienne was
not only an archbishop but a cardinal. Yet he submitted to
election. The example would not have influenced a pious deacon if he could have known de Brienne's later career: how he

was to be denounced by the Pope and stripped of his dignities, would give up his priesthood and within the year die, rumor said, by suicide.

The Barat family, thinking only of their son's safety, urged Louis to take the oath. He hesitated, but in January 1791 he did so. Within a few months the Pope's denunciation of it was published, and Louis could see for himself the violence and abuse in which the oath had resulted. In May 1792 he formally retracted. In nearby Auxerre, priests who did not take the oath were being killed and their bodies left unburied on rubbish heaps as a warning. Louis dodged from one hiding-place to another until, less than a year later, a fellow clerical student denounced him. He was sent to the Paris prisons, five of them in succession, and learned later that he escaped the guillotine only because the man who wrote out the lists of those to be killed was a former schoolmaster of his, who conveniently forgot, time after time, to put down his old pupil's name. In February 1795 he emerged from his last prison, to be ordained priest that autumn and then return to Joigny.

It had not been an experience to soften a man who had the strength to survive it. In Joigny he found Sophie a young girl of fifteen, who had, with the rest of the family, been in danger and sometimes in hiding on account of their relationship with him. She was more subdued than she had been, more convinced that, as she had discovered earlier, no earthly joy is without its shadow. She had known since she was a small child that she wanted to be a nun, preferably a Carmelite. Those strong affections of hers, which had so worried her brother, had always turned as much toward God as toward others, tenderly though she did and always could and would love others. But the years of terror when, released from her brother's training, she had lived through the harder training of circumstances, had taught her this: only God mattered. Nothing less than God's service was worth giving yourself to. She must have admired, even to the point of hero-worship, the persecuted brother languishing in filthy jails, and perhaps, for all they knew, already killed; at any rate, a martyr. She would make an offering, if she could, of no less worth.

Opportunity came at once. Father Louis intended to return to Paris to work clandestinely among the people. Before leaving, he examined the progress of his young sister. She had not given up her books, but had concentrated too much, for his taste, on merely literary studies. She delighted in *Don Quixote;* she had read through *Clarissa Harlowe.* Such frivolity, in a girl who intended to be a nun, did not please Louis. Besides, he noticed that the hard years of anxiety had drawn Sophie and her mother together with such tenderness that he was afraid she would never have the courage to leave her mother or her mother the courage to let her go. He felt responsible for her, as well he might, and he made a suggestion which was just not quite an order. Would she come to Paris with him and continue her studies? She could not enter a convent, because there were no convents, but while waiting to see what God planned for her, she could prepare herself better by living an austere life under his direction in Paris than by remaining in Joigny.

His mother was horrified. She could not live without her younger daughter. This was exactly what Father Louis had expected her to say. What did Sophie think? Sophie, now that her opportunity for being a martyr had come, did not relish the kind of martyrdom proposed. The mind her brother had so carefully trained rushed to draw logical conclusions from incontrovertible premises, and proved that what Louis wanted was not what God wanted. Her main argument was the obvious one that, since she was the only child left at home, even the commandments of God required that she stay and be the comfort of her parents. But she was fighting against herself as well as against him, and in the end she gave way. Her father, much as he would miss her, thought she would be safe in her brother's care, and have more chance of getting on in life. Her mother, conquered though unconvinced, had to submit.

Sophie and her priest brother went up to Paris with a girl of Sophie's own age. The two girls tried to brighten the boredom of the three-day trip by chattering together. But Louis gave his sister a foretaste of what life in his company was to be like by pointing out that such trivial talk was poor preparation for coming to a city red with the blood of recent martyrs, where religion was still persecuted.

Brother and sister settled in the house of an elderly unmarried lady, Mademoiselle Duval, in the Rue de Touraine. One room was arranged as a chapel where Louis could say his Mass, and a few neighbors came in to attend it. Two of them were to figure in Sophie's later experience: a literary and strong-minded, though not very organized lady, called Mademoiselle Loquet, and Octavie Bailly, a girl from Rouen, who was living in Paris now with her widowed mother and older sister. During the Terror, the Bailly women had, besides working to earn their living, helped hunted priests, brought them to give the sacraments to the dying, taught children religion—always at the risk of their lives. Octavie was ten years older than Sophie, but both shared the temporarily futile desire to be nuns.

Father Louis thought the best thing he could do, besides
guiding their attempts at prayer and spiritual improvement,
was to educate them, since, in such times, nuns prepared to
teach would be doubly useful. With Mademoiselle Duval as
chaperone, he began lessons for the three young ladies. Sophie
was far ahead of the others, but he made her go slowly, because
he thought it was good for her patience, as indeed it was. While
she shared her secular studies with the others, she was being
put through a much stiffer course in the Scriptures, in theology,
in the Fathers and Doctors of the Church. It was her familiarity
with these that gave such solidity and balance to her own spiritual life and to her later teaching, preserving them from every
hint of sentimentality and giving an intellectually sound basis
for her devotion.

She was sixteen when she began her four years in Paris with
her brother. She was completing her education, but hardly as
a girl would today in college. In the first place, the two were
poor. He gave lessons to earn a little money. She did sewing
for the same purpose, helped with the housework, and had
pupils of her own, who idolized her, as children always had
idolized her. But they could afford no pleasures (not that
Father Louis would have allowed them if they could) and
sometimes had scarcely enough to eat. These were minor in-
conveniences by comparison with her brother's way of directing her conscience. A robust and unimaginative man, he had
no suspicion that long, scrupulous examinations of conscience
could be a torture for her. He treated minor faults as if they
were grave sins, and so frightened her that she did not dare,
sometimes, to go to Communion until he ordered her to. Once,
fearing God even more than she feared her brother, she ate

something before Mass so that he could not force her to receive the sacrament. That she survived all this, and even continued to be fond of Louis, shows that she had in her, under
her sensitivity, not a little of his vein of iron. Perhaps he saw
this. If he did, he relied on it more than ordinary prudence
could justify, but she came through.

There were brief periods of respite when, keeping a promise
made to their mother, she went home to Joigny. We have a
description of her at this time given later by a nephew, her
sister's son, who became a priest. He remembered how, when
he was a very small boy, he had gone out for walks with her,
and how she told him stories and recited verse for him as they
wandered along the banks of the Yonne. Once he forgot he had
a butterfly cupped in his hands, and let it escape because he
was so distracted by his pleasure in what she was saying, or by
the charm of her voice as she said it, or perhaps only by her
kindness. The charm was felt by others older than he. She was
an attractive girl, whose intelligent alertness never made anyone else feel inferior. She went out to others and thought more
of them than of herself. How far she believed the low estimate
of her that her brother kept repeating is hard to tell. At any
rate, the repetition and her scruples prevented her taking any
pleasure in her superiority if, as is doubtful, she was aware
of it.

Toward the end of these four years, she finally came to terms
with her situation. Though her brother was still letting her
overwork, trying her vanity by insisting that she wear her
peasant costume in Paris, and even tearing up or throwing into
the fire pretty things she made for herself and presents she
made for him, she had learned two ways of keeping her equa-

nimity. One, very characteristic, was by laughing at herself and
him, though not unkindly and never out loud. The other was
by prayer. Her genius was always a genius for personal relations. Somehow—partly from Louis himself—she had come to
know that God was more than a lawgiver who thundered from
Mount Sinai, though she knew He was that, and though she
insisted all her life that children be taught the fear of God and
the horror of sin. But to her, when she could forget the anxie-
ties stirred up by Father Barat's rigor, God was a loving God
who had become man to make it easier for men to obey His
laws, and to save them from sin's consequences when they dis-
obeyed. A Person who was both God and man had suffered to
win a way of escape for men because He loved them. This was
what Sophie knew, and this was the conviction on which she
was to base her life with such stubborn consistency, backed up
by such intellectual clarity and such intense love, that she became a saint and was recognized as a saint before her life was
half over. The special form her sanctity took was decided, after
her four years in Paris, by what seemed a chance meeting with
a man as extraordinary as herself.

CHAPTER TWO

1800–1802

Paris to Amiens

That man was Joseph Varin. He was Louis Barat's age, but he had had a more colorful career. Converted from a youthful passion for horses, hunts and racing, he had spent three years at the famous seminary of Saint Sulpice in Paris, where he ruined his health by such imprudences as going for a whole week without sleep while preparing for a philosophy examination, and by what his biographer calls "an immoderate use of coffee." He left the seminary and the city on the day the Bastille fell, promptly signed up with the forces fighting against the revolutionists, and found army life agreed with him better than the seminary. In July 1794, when he had almost forgotten his earlier ambitions, he met some former seminary companions in Belgium, and allowed himself to be persuaded to join them in a new religious congregation. He later learned that on the day after he made this decision, his mother had been guillotined in Paris. Among the four friends was Léonor de Tournély, a remarkably holy young man, who became superior when the little group formed themselves into an association called the Fathers of the Sacred Heart. After leaving Belgium, they spent five weeks walking to Germany, and there, after two years, Joseph Varin was ordained priest by the uncle of Louis XVI.

One of Father de Tournély's projects was a society of women, who would also be consecrated to the Sacred Heart, and would cooperate with the Fathers by teaching girls of the higher classes. De Tournély was very clear about what God wanted. These women were to reawaken the love of Jesus Christ in the soul, and the light of His teaching in the mind, by "putting on the mind of Christ," by sharing the thoughts and attitudes of Christ and trying to make others share them. A Princess of Bourbon-Condé seemed at one time an excellent choice for foundress. She was willing, gathered some ex-nuns around her, and formed a new institute, but soon retired to the Trappistines (and soon left them) while her companions scattered. De Tournély, disappointed, nevertheless confided to Father Varin his prophetic certainty that, though he did not know when or how, the society of women would be founded. Before he died in 1797, at the age of thirty, he entrusted to Varin, who succeeded him as superior, his favorite plan. Varin soon found a pious archduchess, sister of the Emperor of Germany, and she, with two of her ladies in waiting named Naudet, tried another foundation. This was more lasting, but in the end, through rather complicated circumstances, proved not to be the society of de Tournély's hopes.

The Fathers of the Sacred Heart, who had increased in number during the years in Germany, really wanted to be Jesuits. The Society of Jesus, however, had been suppressed by the Holy See a quarter of a century before, and survived only in Russia. Nevertheless, the would-be Jesuits hoped it might be restored in time for them to become sons of Saint Ignatius.

Shortly after de Tournély's death, the Pope suggested that they join a group called the Fathers of the Faith under the Italian Paccanari. Since the Pope wished it, they could hardly refuse, and the archduchess with her nuns was also placed under Paccanari's authority. Eventually, by his influence, the tone and purpose of the women's group changed.

In June 1800, Father Varin with two of his companions, now Fathers of the Faith, had returned to Paris where they met Philibert de Bruillard, a young priest from Dijon. During the Terror, he had been one of seven priests who, one on each day of the week, followed the carts bringing the condemned to the guillotine and secretly gave each victim conditional absolution just before death. Bruillard, who later became Bishop of Grenoble, was a friend of Louis Barat, and had for a time been Sophie's spiritual director. He introduced the two priests, and Louis at once asked to join the Fathers of the Faith. Father Varin, as local superior, inquired into the applicant's responsibilities, and heard about the younger sister, who was, at the time, in Joigny. Father Varin had some doubts about Paccanari, and was beginning to feel that a German archduchess in a convent in Rome was not the best instrument for educating young ladies in France. He listened, therefore, with considerable interest to the description of Sophie. She was twenty. She wanted to be a nun. She was extremely intelligent and unusually well educated. Here, Father Varin saw, was what he wanted. He received Louis as a Father of the Faith and suggested that he might have plans for Sophie.

After a month at home Sophie returned to Paris, and Father Varin met her. He was struck by her modesty, her timidity, her physical frailty, but he saw also how she could be trained, and he made up his mind on the spot. Louis, whom he consulted, fell in with his plans, glad to transfer his sister to the authority of his new superior. For Sophie's spiritual life it was not a second but a first spring. There was nothing soft or undecided about Joseph Varin, and when he was convinced of God's Will, he could act with force and authority. But he was also gentle, and could adapt himself to characters and temperaments unlike his own, because he respected their freedom and God's plans for them. His methods were positive. His motto, "Courage and confidence!" he repeated in season and out. After her years of subjection to rigor and self-examination, nothing could have been more suited to Sophie Barat's spiritual needs. Her brother's treatment had tended to break in her what might turn to evil. Father Varin's work was to build up her faith in herself, to train her to trust her judgment and act on it, but always to have blind trust in God and follow unhesitatingly wherever He called.

Before telling Sophie where he thought God was calling her now, he prayed to be sure the plan was really God's. When he was sure, he asked her one day what she intended to do with her life. She said she had always wanted to be a nun, and thought her vocation was for the Carmelites. Carmelites, as Father Varin knew, led a life of heroic penance through love for Jesus Christ, and such an attraction was just what a member of his Society of the Sacred Heart needed. He told her he knew a way in which she could have what she wanted. But instead of laying down the law at once, as she was accustomed to have her brother do, he spoke at some length about the intellectual training she had received, insinuating that, given such preparation, she should follow a path more suited for the times than seclusion behind the iron grill of a completely cloistered convent. God had inspired her brother to teach her. God must have intended that she teach others. He told her the story of Léonor de Tournély's hopes and predictions, and mentioned the foundation in Rome. There was, however, urgent work to be done in France, and he was sure she was meant to do it.

Sophie was not prepared to give an immediate answer, though the picture he drew, since it included prayer as well as sacrifice, was attractive. She said she would think about it. But the aristocratic young priest from Besançon, who had been a dragoon officer, had not lost his power of command. There was no necessity, he said, for further thinking. When God wanted something, and you saw He did, you obeyed. Sophie was a little surprised, but she was used to obeying. She said she would this time, too.

Her habit of giving in when anyone with the slightest authority spoke may seem—did, as a matter of fact, seem to some of her contemporaries—a form of weakness. It was as if her brother's treatment had broken something in her which was never mended. Even Father Varin himself spoke of her "timidity." Was she afraid of facing decisions, or merely apathetically resigned? Anyone who thought this of her then or later (and she was still being accused of it when she was sixty) knew little of her or of saints in general. Her obedience was an active recognition of God's voice speaking to her through those who bore His mandate. She did not give in passively, but went forward with love to meet what she saw as the Will of God. Obedience was a joy, even when it demanded costly personal sacrifice.

Army life had given Father Varin skill in rapid organization. His small platoon was ready. There were four to start with.

Octavie Bailly, in spite of her active service during the Terror, or perhaps because of it, still looked longingly to the peace of the cloister, but she promised to join the new enterprise because she found it hard to say *no*, as people were always to find it hard to say *no*, when Sophie Barat wanted anything. And Sophie, once she was used to the idea, wanted this apostolic life very much. She was especially delighted by the prospect of consecration to the Sacred Heart, which meant to the love of God made man. Father Varin had spoken to her, in terms more familiar to us than they were to her, of how this devotion to love had been revealed by God only in "these last days," and was designed to break through the winter of skepticism that had descended on France. It was the mission of the Church, he had pointed out to her, to spread the shining of the Heart of Christ, which would provide both the light of faith and the warmth of love and devotion. If the work was to be done, the Church needed her children, including her daughters.

These high thoughts had found good fuel in Sophie's mind and heart. Octavie, dazzled by the glow of it, could not resist. Marguerite Maillard, Mademoiselle Duval's servant, who had also known Sophie long enough to be charmed by her, asked if she might come in, too. She could not teach, but she was a skilled dressmaker, and that was an essential accomplishment in any group of women. The fourth in the group was the redoubtable Mademoiselle Loquet. Father Varin accepted her a little glumly. She was highly thought of by the clergy and had some small renown as the author of pious allegorical works, including one called *The Voyage of Sophie and Eulalia to the Palace of Happiness*. Father Varin was no literary critic, but his experience had made him think well of the theory that God

chooses the weak things of this world to confound the strong. He said of Mademoiselle Loquet that he could do with a little less celebrity. However, Father Barat may have championed his mature student, and the superior submitted to his apparently better judgment. The lady kept her independence, up to a point, by coming to the house in the Rue de Touraine only for Father Varin's instructions, whereas the other three lived there, under regulations devised by him, working and praying together and having nothing to do with the world outside their doors.

In the early instructions, given usually in the morning after Mass, Father Varin sketched for his not quite homogeneous quartet the main outlines of the institute he planned. There was one center of the structure round which all the parts were arranged. This was that neither their own sanctification nor the salvation of souls was the aim and end of the institute. The aim was to give glory to the Sacred Heart. Everything else, no matter how important, was a means to that end. It was Sophie who understood this aim so clearly that she was always able to detect any deviation from it in the substitute plans later suggested to her.

Sometimes Father Varin's instructions took the form of conversation. All agreed that the spirit of the institute was to be one of generosity. The service of the Sacred Heart demanded strong souls who could yet be gentle, intrepid souls who were willing to be humbled. If a strong, generous love of Jesus Christ was essential to the work, the workers must root pettiness out of their lives. They could not afford those faults in which men think women particularly indulge, especially when they live together in small groups: sensitiveness, brooding over slights,

irrational likes and dislikes. They must not be cowards, must not allow themselves the luxury of wanting and not wanting at the same time. But if they were to fulfill their vocation as Father Varin saw it, there were two other things, apparently mutually exclusive, which they must learn to do at the same time: praying and working. They must belong completely to Christ and completely to souls.

Sophie, for all her Carmelite leanings, found herself suddenly on fire to be a missionary, especially when a priest about to set out for Madagascar urged them to devote themselves to the infidels. It was an ambition that died hard in her; but she kept it as an ideal for the society that was beginning, and lived to see it gloriously carried out. But for herself she was told: "No, your work is in France."

While Father Varin was preparing the new enterprise, he was not neglecting his own responsibilities as superior of the Fathers of the Faith. Priests were by now allowed to carry on their ministry more freely, though churches were still closed, and the Archbishop of Paris welcomed these ardent new recruits. They were soon working day and night in prisons and hospitals. The field was white for the harvest and most of the laborers who had not died under the guillotine knife were in exile. Father Varin alone conducted missions for thousands in the hospitals, baptized two hundred teen-age boys and prepared five hundred more for confirmation. What had Madagascar to offer that Paris had not? It was God, of course, who was giving the increase, but the priest's personality partly accounted for the speed with which the grain sprang up. Among people unsettled by long fear or sickened by their own excesses, he could be reassuring or commanding, as the case required.

He swept obstacles out of his way without either losing his composure or standing on his dignity. De Tournély had told him once that he would always be a soldier, and he was, combining a comrade's good-natured tolerance with an officer's power of command.

From this prodigious activity, he came back daily to the four in the Rue de Touraine. He had first met Sophie Barat in the spring of 1800. By November, he was ready to let her and her companions make some formal offering of themselves to the service of God. After he was sure they wanted to, he told them they could do so on the twenty-first of November, when the Church celebrates the tradition that the Mother of God was brought to the Temple as a small child, and left there to learn to serve God. It was an appropriate feast. After giving them a few days of preparatory prayer, he said Mass on the morning of the twenty-first before a picture of Mary and her Child in the tiny chapel. The picture is still honored in the Mother House of the Society of the Sacred Heart in Rome. The Child is the typically chubby and curly and rather large infant dear to nineteenth-century taste, but the Mother is exquisite. She is sitting, dressed in a robe of dark orange shading into red, with a darker cloak thrown over her head and showing a pale lining. Her head is inclined toward the clinging Child, and her expression is almost sadly grave.

There is some doubt as to whether some or all of the four were allowed to make a formal consecration to the Sacred Heart. Of the four, at any rate, it was only Sophie Barat and Marguerite Maillard who persevered, and all her life Sophie remembered this day as a wife remembers the day of her engagement. She was twenty. She knew finally, after years of uncertainty, what way God wanted her to follow. She had never seen a nun in her life and therefore the details of her future were not at all clear to her; but details were unimportant.

After this, they settled down again to their simple, laborious life. Mademoiselle Loquet, whether from want of space or more pressing obligations, still came in only occasionally. This spasmodic appearance prevented Father Varin and the others from knowing as much about her as life together might have revealed. Father Varin himself was away much of the time, for he and his priests were extending their ministry to other parts of the country. Almost a year passed in this fashion. Sophie, left increasingly to her own meditations, was slowly working out for herself what her happy consecration implied.

Devotion to the Sacred Heart was not, for her, a new devotion. Louis had sent home from Paris a picture of the Sacred Heart. Now, with Father Varin's urging that she examine her conscience less and think of God more, she brought to her meditation all the deep thoughts with which she had become familiar in reading the Fathers of the Church. The pierced Heart of Jesus Christ on Calvary, she came more and more clearly to see, explained all the theology of the Redemption. From it flowed the Water and Blood, symbol of the love which must bring the world back to God. Until now she had, perhaps, thought too much of how men—including Sophie Barat—had sinned. Now she saw that the love in the Heart of Christ was a fire more violent than the fire of Hell prepared for sinners. To save sinners she had only to let herself be set on fire with the love He had come on earth to kindle. If she did this, by suffering anything He wanted her to suffer, she could save others from their sins, whether she worked for them directly or only prayed for them. It did not matter, then, what work she might be put to, for whatever she did under obedience would help set the world on fire with His Love.

In the summer of 1801 she went back to Joigny for her last holiday, which lasted until well into the autumn. Louis was with her there for part of the time. It is uncertain whether their mother knew how definite the break had been made, but Father Louis was not one to soften blows. There were still to be brief visits later, but Joigny was no longer home.

Late in the autumn the new work began.

In May 1801, Father Varin went to Amiens in Picardy to preach a retreat and to open a school for boys. Napoleon was working out a Concordat with the Pope, and there was high hope that religion might soon again be freely practised. Besides, because the people of Amiens did not hold with the killing of priests and the closing of churches, and because even the courts were lukewarm in enforcing anti-religious legislation, the city had been a place of refuge during even the worst periods of persecution. The churches remained open, though often in the hands of priests who had taken the civil oath, and for the many faithful who did not recognize such priests, there were private chapels where non-jurors celebrated Mass. Religious ousted from other cities or flying from persecution were welcome in Amiens, and when new congregations began to be formed after the Concordat was signed, many had their beginnings there.

Father Varin met a priest named Antoine Bicheron, who had been driven from his own diocese of Soissons by the Revolution and taken shelter in Amiens, where he began a school for young noblemen. Father Varin spoke to his new friend of the young ladies in the Rue de Touraine. Interested, Father Bicheron suggested the names of two young women who might like to join the four in Paris. The first was Geneviève Deshayes, thirty-four years old, orphaned but well provided for, who lived with her married brother. She had a weakness for pretty clothes and for society, but she loved God and the poor, and shared Father Bicheron's devotion for the Sacred Heart. Like Octavie Bailly and others who were to join the new Society, she had, during the Revolution, worked much for priests and religious, although, in hospitable Amiens, the work was more one of placing and supporting refugees than of hiding fugitives. She was still giving time and money to works of charity, but now that the country was quieter was looking for some settled way of serving God.

When Father Bicheron advised her to consult Father Varin, she found him in lodgings barer than a military barrack, furnished with a camp bed and one chair. He spoke only of the Sacred Heart. It was not until a few months later, in August, that he told her the history and aims of the new Society. The group in Rome, who were called the Diletti di Gesu were still the main branch, but he described for her the four in Paris, especially Sophie Barat. Then he said, with the decision customary to him when he had prayed over something and was sure he was right, that God meant her to join them. From that moment, she admitted later, she felt as if she had come into a house made expressly for her and to her taste, but without her knowledge.

The other young lady Father Bicheron directed to Father Varin was a friend of Geneviève, Henriette Grosier, who shared with Sophie and Octavie the desire for a contemplative life in

Carmel. The new Society was explained to her as Carmel plus direct work with and for souls. She was not difficult to persuade, but she had one problem. What was she to do about her elderly aunt, a nun who had been driven from her convent, and who was now, with Henriette, running a boarding school for girls in the city? The school was not going too well, but schools were so necessary at the moment that it hardly seemed right to abandon it.

Everyone except the aunt thought that the perfect solution would be to turn the school over to the new Society. Mademoiselle Loquet was sent for from Paris to join the staff of the school and learn its customs. She was to be Superior, and Geneviève Deshayes was impressed by Father Varin's account of her talents and literary fame. She arrived early in September, and there ensued a painful few weeks during which the learned but impatient author tried to persuade Henriette's reluctant aunt to cede the establishment to the newcomers. After much backtracking and indecision, Father Bicheron intervened between the two ladies and worked out an understanding, which was drawn up in the form of a contract and signed at nine o'clock on the evening of October 15, feast of St. Teresa, who seemed, by the coincidence, to be, with her accustomed graciousness, yielding possible Carmelites to the more pressing needs of His Majesty, her Lord.

The school was on a street called Martin Bleu-Dieu, where a man named Martin had a statue of God the Father in a blue robe. The house was not handsome. On the first floor there was a disproportionately large entrance hall with a kitchen and another tiny room on one side, two larger rooms which would serve for classrooms on the other, and a small garden, adorned with a single tree for shade, behind. The sleeping rooms were above, and on the top floor a chapel was fitted out in the attic. On October 17, anniversary of the death of Margaret Mary Alacoque, Mademoiselle Loquet, with Geneviève and Henriette, formally assumed possession of the premises and responsibility for the twenty pupils. Sophie Barat and her brother were in Joigny until late September, when a letter from Father Varin announced that Octavie was waiting to join Sophie in Paris and proceed with her to Amiens to help out the small staff there. Accompanied by Marguerite Maillard, Octavie and Sophie set out on the first of Sophie's hundreds of weary journeys in bad coaches over ill-kept roads deep in mud, with far from restful stops at primitive inns. About the middle of November they reached the little town where, in the next few years, the number of saints walking the cobblestoned streets would rival the number of those crowding the pedestals of the superb cathedral.

Geneviève Deshayes, by now recovered from the tearful scenes attending her departure from her prostrate family, was awaiting with keen interest the arrival of this girl thirteen years younger than herself, about whose virtue and learning Father Varin had been eloquent. She was won at sight by Sophie's charm and modesty. To inaugurate the new venture Father Varin preached a retreat. Its theme was "God alone!" and thirty years later Mother Barat still could reminisce about it with Mother Grosier. When it was over, the retreat master asked whether all were determined to remain in the Society, and wished to renew their pledge to do so. Octavie Bailly found she still thought of Carmel. The rest, in the chapel of the house where Father Varin was staying, made their offering on November 21, just a year after the first ceremony in the Rue de Touraine. By an accident later seen as prophetic, Sophie, who was to make her promise last, made it first. Father Varin preached on the text: "Blessed art thou that hast believed, because those things shall be accomplished that were spoken to thee by the Lord."

The new society was temporarily referred to as the Ladies of Christian Instruction, for they could not as yet call themselves the Society of the Sacred Heart. Because Royalists in the Vendée had carried badges of the Sacred Heart when they fought against the revolutionists, the name was regarded with suspicion. People had been executed for simply giving away badges of the Sacred Heart.

The business of daily living had to be arranged. Octavie was sent to the Diletti in Rome to decide what she wanted. Father Varin set out again on his missionary journeys. The school in Rue Martin Bleu-Dieu was left under the care of the other Fathers of the Faith from their school in the Rue de l'Oratoire. With Mademoiselle Loquet at the head of the establishment, work began. Sophie and Henriette Grosier conducted the higher classes, and Sophie also taught religion to the younger children. Geneviève, who said she had forgotten everything she ever knew, was appointed to drill the more backward children in reading. As a group, the twenty pupils were hard to manage. They did not, as Geneviève later remarked, "take to" Mademoiselle Loquet, and this made life a little difficult. She taught religion to the higher classes, using her allegorical tales as texts, but Geneviève notes that her teaching was over their heads. Perhaps her young audience was not up to allegory.

If the house was a Palace of Happiness for the overworked

young teachers, it was because they had the Blessed Sacrament with them in the attic chapel, although Mass was seldom said there. Mademoiselle Loquet's direction could hardly have added to their bliss. She still kept somewhat aloof from the rest, even sleeping on another floor, and rapping on their ceiling at five o'clock to wake them up for the day. But miscellaneous noises were sometimes mistaken for this ambiguous signal, and the sleepy young nuns were occasionally up and dressed by three. Then followed an hour of prayer, the best hour of the day. Father Varin had taught them to say "Magister adest," whenever they were summoned to rise or go to their duties. "The Master is here and calleth for thee," Martha had said to her sister Mary, and Sophie and her companions imitated the speed with which Mary had run to throw herself at the feet of her Master. With Him they gathered strength for the strenuous day ahead.

Geneviève, who did not have the advantage of having been trained by Louis Barat, found it specially strenuous, in ways that probably did not bother Sophie. She suffered agonies when she had to sweep the street stairs, where she might be observed by her former friends. Mademoiselle Loquet had devised a costume for them so odd that when they accompanied their pupils to high Mass at the parish church, they were stared at by the distracted congregation. In the same dress they took their little girls for walks, not in the quieter sections but, by Mademoiselle Loquet's orders, along the main street, where Geneviève's friends no doubt stationed themselves dutifully to see what a frump the elegant young lady had turned herself into for the love of God. All the beautifully frilled and flounced gowns of her past were being gradually sold, together with small articles of furniture and other possessions her weeping family had pressed upon her when she left home, for the financial situation of the school was precarious.

So straitened were they that there was not even enough to eat. They ate in silence what was left over from the pupils' meals, while one of them read out solemnly the collected works of Mademoiselle Loquet, not only the *Voyage of Sophie and Eulalia,* but the *Conversation of Clothilde and Angelica,* and other gems of allegory from which they might cull fragments for their teaching. When the children were in bed, and Mademoiselle Loquet had retired to her private—though also poor —apartment to try to balance her books, her small community gathered happily about the kitchen fire, sewing to earn money for their support, and talking of their wish to go on the foreign missions. At least, Sophie and Henriette wanted to go. At this early stage, Geneviève thought she would rather stay in France, whatever the humiliation of being so close to family and friends.

One of the most delightful idylls of the early years of the Society is this interlude, half comic and half sublime, when, less than half a dozen in all, they submitted obediently and even joyously to the haphazard, arbitrary government of a well-meaning lady utterly unfitted for religious life. There may be something naïve in the picture of Geneviève Deshayes sitting of an evening in the little kitchen, playing on her harp the accompaniment she had written for the psalm: "How good it is for brothers to dwell together in unity!" while her companions bent over their needle work. But there was nothing naïve or unreal about the serenity with which so intelligent a young woman as Sophie Barat took it for granted that Mademoiselle

Loquet's erratic commands were, for her, the Will of God. This episode is, as a matter of fact, central to the whole story of Madeleine Sophie Barat's life. For it shows her, in a situation ludicrous to the unsympathetic observer, putting into action the principle by which she lived. She did not distrust her own intelligence or lack attachment to her own will. She was simply convinced that God loved her, and that she had sufficient reason to believe He was speaking to her through Mademoiselle Loquet because that lady was her legitimately appointed superior.

Reports describe Sophie, at this time, as so absorbed in prayer that she would not have cared what she was told to do. Geneviève and Henriette, less detached from circumstances, would have preferred that she show herself more aware of their peculiar situation. All we know of her thoughts at this time we guess from Father Varin's letters to her, assuring her that God loves her, is not angry at her faults, and wants her to be happy and at peace. She was already engaged in the typical saint's struggle to reconcile herself to what she is, knowing how far short it falls of what she might be. This vision of perfection does not disturb the rest of the world because it is seen only by those who come dangerously close to God. "Man cannot see God and live" is a maxim that can be read in several ways. God's nearness is not dangerous to what is good or even "natural," in the best sense, in man. It is dangerous only to what keeps man from being his deepest self, that is, from being what God intended him to be. Saints come so close to God that they see more and more exactly what He wants; and so they are appalled by what look to others like grains of dust. What Sophie's "faults" were we have no way of knowing. They might easily have been moments of recognition that Mademoiselle Loquet was being imprudent or tyrannical. In one revealing sentence of his letter, Father Varin tells her she must let nothing which "our dear brother Barat" has said to her cause her worry or weaken her courage and joy.

The situation lasted eighteen months. Geneviève Deshayes soon gave up teaching and devoted herself to being sacristan, taking care of the others when they were ill, and sewing for the pupils. Mademoiselle Loquet sometimes embarrassed her with confidences about how she disagreed with Father Varin's ideas. The Superior was also over-indulgent to her niece, who was one of the pupils, and to that valuable person, the convent cook. The niece was allowed to toss water glasses in the air, and the cook to waste the precious, not very plentiful food. The cook slept in the warmest part of the sleeping room, whereas the others were placed in a draught from the badly closed door. Of all this, which Geneviève later wrote down, there was no discussion whatever among Mademoiselle Loquet's subjects at the time, and the priest Father Varin had left as adviser to the convent was not bothered by the Superior's peculiarities.

Several important changes occurred in these months. At the beginning of 1802, a single-roomed separate building nearby was hired as a school for poor children, and soon housed one hundred and sixty of them. This increased work the little community took in their stride. The children were divided into groups. Those who knew more were deputed to teach those who knew less, or at least to hear them recite the lessons taught by the nuns. The children were considerably more docile and responsive than the boarding school pupils, who were led astray by the changeable tactics of Mademoiselle Loquet and the

bad example of her niece. Once, when Sophie and Geneviève
took the boarders out for a walk, they decided to run away and
had to be pursued along the streets by breathless Sister Sophie
while Geneviève held on by main force to those who had not
yet escaped. After this sort of performance, it was relaxing to
deal with the grateful poor children.

In April of the same year, three others who wished to join
the Society came to make the growing burden more bearable.
One was Adèle Jugon, a vigorous, able girl of great personal
charm and dignity, who, before she was twenty-five, had carried
on an apostolate in her native village so sweepingly successful
as to make convent life, even under Mademoiselle Loquet,
tame. She stayed only a short time in Amiens, left to marry a
wealthy nobleman who died and bequeathed her a fortune, and
spent her last years lavishing it to cure every misery she could
discover about her. During the short time she stayed in the
Rue Martin Bleu-Dieu, she made life happier for everyone
concerned.

The other arrivals were two former Poor Clares, Claude Capy
and Anne Baudemont. Madame Baudemont was accepted
rather reluctantly by Father Varin, whose vision of what
Father de Tournély had planned for the Society made him
adept at spotting possible misfits. A woman of great power and
administrative ability, who had done heroic works of charity
during the revolution, Anne Baudemont wanted originally
to revive the Order of the Poor Clares, and introduce into it
certain reforms. When she read a highly impressive article
about the Roman Diletti, and wrote to Father Varin asking to
join their French sisters, he pointed out difficulties. If she felt
called to reform a great Order, she could hardly also have a

call to become a humble member of a new, small congregation.
There were ecclesiastical permissions required before she could
move from the Poor Clares (even though her convent had been
suppressed) to a group not yet approved by the Church. He
advised her to think longer about her position.

She was not put off, however, and he finally gave permission
for her and her companion to go to Amiens while waiting to be
dispensed from their former obligations. A possible reason for
her interest was that Father Nicholas Loriquet, who was to
become the great organizer of Jesuit studies, had just joined
the Fathers of the Faith and been assigned to their school in
Amiens. Madame Baudemont had become very attached to
Loriquet when he was imprisoned in Rheims, and had actually
saved his life. When a plan was afoot for helping him escape
prison and the death sentence, she had gone to the chief
member of the tribunal, an honest but weak and timid man,
and browbeaten him (in a way "which had nothing feminine
about it," says the Father's biographer), into offering his
own house as a hiding place until better could be arranged.

Early in June Father Varin made one of his infrequent
visits, and allowed Geneviève and Sophie to make their vows.
Henriette Grosier had some doubts about her own wishes, and
Father Varin evidently had doubts about Mademoiselle Loquet.
On the morning of June 7, Pentecost Monday, the ceremony
was to take place in the chapel of the Fathers of the Faith.
When it was time to leave the house on Rue Martin Bleu-Dieu,
Sophie did not appear, and was found after some search in the
garden, so deep in prayer that it was at first difficult to get her
attention.

Ten days later, the growing community moved to a new

house on Rue Neuve. The moving took place at six o'clock in the evening on the popular feast of the Blessed Sacrament, just when the streets were filled. Each one loaded herself down with all she could carry, and all marched together through the gaping crowd, providing an extra spectacle for the holiday. The new house had no grounds, and a little place outside town was hired where the children could be taken for country air. It was usually Sophie who took them, with Adèle Jugon, who was taller and had a stronger voice, to help her call out or run after them when they fled.

An even more important event occurred in this busy month. Father Varin was by now seriously bothered by what he had observed of Mademoiselle Loquet in action. Fortunately, one of the Diletti, Madame Louise Naudet, was sent from Rome just then to see how the French house was progressing. Father Varin, who was to be in Rome during the time of her visitation, decided to use her visit to test the conclusions he was drawing. He warned her before she began that she was facing a difficult situation for which she would need the help of God. She soon received frank descriptions of the chaotic state of things from Madame Baudemont, and from Adèle Jugon, who knew she did not intend to remain and wished to do a final service to her companions.

An experienced and intelligent woman, Madame Naudet was appalled by the mismanagement she saw. Before making any decision, she invited the community to join her in a novena to Our Lady before the feast of the Assumption, a novena with such happy results that it became a tradition—still preserved—in the Society. It was Mother Barat who made it a tradition, and her doing so is our best clue to how clearly she saw the ill effects of Mademoiselle Loquet's government. All she would ever say about that lady was that "she did not have the spirit of the Society," but she admitted that unless some sweeping reform had been introduced, the Society "would have perished." The result of the novena was Madame Naudet's decision to write her opinion of Mademoiselle Loquet to Father Varin. He wrote back that he would come as soon as possible and take strong measures. He arrived in November, and spoke to Mademoiselle Loquet with his usual openness. She decided to withdraw and did so on December 3, pursued by only one anxiety: that there was obviously no one left who was qualified to take her place.

Others did not share her anxiety. There is evidence in Father Varin's letter to Madame Naudet that she had suggested Sister Sophie as Superior. Adèle Jugon had said Sophie was obviously best suited for this position. The visitor discreetly inquired of the rest what their views were, and found that they were her own. Her one objection to Sister Sophie was that her health was so poor. Deciding this came from her effort to be always conscious of God's presence, she made the girl's life miserable by ordering her to distract herself from the thought of God— the identical order which had once, for the same reason, been given to St. Aloysius Gonzaga. On December 20, she called the community together and spoke to them of how absolutely they must devote themselves to the apostolate. Addressing herself to Sophie, she said severely that she, for one, must really *come out of herself*. Sophie knelt down and said: "Shall I ever be allowed to go back?" Everyone burst out laughing, and Sister Deshayes, who tells the story, was delighted. Next morning, Father Varin went to the convent, spoke to the nuns, and said that to judge how fitted they were for teaching the young he was going to ask some questions. After a few minutes, he turned to Sophie and said that, since she was the youngest, he would ask her the easiest question: why had God made her? She answered: to know, love and serve Him. He continued: what does it mean to serve God? Sophie said: to do His Will. That was what he had been waiting for.

"I hope," he said, "that *you* want to do God's Will?" She said she did. "Well, God's Will is that you should be Superior."

"It almost cost her her life," Father Varin impenitently observed when he told the story. "For ten years she kept begging for mercy. Happily for her daughters, she was only wasting her time."

Father Varin, nonetheless, could feel for her. He had accepted his own election as Superior with the same reluctance.

Mother Barat was twenty-three. The burden just laid on her she was to carry for almost sixty-three years.

CHAPTER THREE

1802–1804

Superior at Amiens

A saint's terror at the thought of being a religious Superior often seems unreal to the onlooker. After all, says common sense, everyone would rather give orders than take them. Isn't it merely coy to pretend you don't like others to defer to you? The answer is that an honest and intelligent man knows he is apt to like it, and that if he is a saint he also knows that almost nothing can do him and his subjects more harm than his liking to give orders and be deferred to.

In Madeleine Sophie Barat's life there recur frequent expressions of her incapacity, and of her hope that others will see how badly she does her job and will relieve her of it. When she was first named Superior, she was replacing a woman who, as Mother Barat was well aware, had almost ruined the infant organization by her own defects. Yet Mademoiselle Loquet had been a pious, estimable, even efficient person, who went back to her charitable works among the poor in Paris, and accomplished great things for God. It was not, then, enough to be pious, to be well-intentioned, even to be efficient. What was necessary? Mother Barat, young though she was, understood exactly what was necessary. A religious Superior, if she was to be of any real use, especially at the beginning of a congregation, had to regard herself habitually and with conviction as the tool of God, Whose work she was doing, and had to keep herself so aware of the relationship that she instinctively asked His direction in every move.

What was there about this twenty-three-year-old girl which had made women, all older than herself and some much more experienced, judge her capable of directing them? She was, in the first place, decidedly the best educated, and that was to be considered in a teaching congregation. But then Mademoiselle Loquet also had had considerable talent. Mother Barat was probably chosen not for her learning but because she had qualities the opposite of Mademoiselle Loquet's. She was lovable, very hard on herself and thoughtful of others, and not only given to prayer but visibly occupied with the thought of God whenever immediate business did not distract her. Women who had already lived religious life or were coming to it full of the highest ideals would not be unimpressed by such indications that Sister Sophie could become a channel of God to them.

For two years, Mother Barat had the fairly close cooperation of Father Varin, who was usually away but kept up an active correspondence with the young Superior. Much of this was concerned with the young—and sometimes not so young— women whom he sent to join the staff of her struggling school. He soon found out, to his amusement and no doubt to his satisfaction, that she had her own views on candidates for the religious life, and was not willing to accept everyone he and the other Fathers of the Faith sent to her. She held out valiantly against one, who was not gifted with much intelligence, but finally gave in with the remark that since they were now nine in the community, she supposed they must have at least one zero if they were to be ten, and the lady proposed was undoubtedly a zero. Luckily, the zero later left of her own accord, and Mother Barat, recalling the incident, remarked that Father Varin learned in time that a candidate for a teaching order must have *something* inside her head.

Several of the newcomers had a great deal. One was the daughter of the astronomer Cassini, a brilliant but volatile girl, who could not teach anything but science. She left the Society for a while but later returned and stayed. Another was a Mademoiselle de Terrail, a former pupil of the school founded in the seventeenth century at St. Cyr by Madame de Maintenon, and a descendant of Bayard, that fearless and irreproachable knight whose description has become a cliché. A third was Henriette Ducis, niece of the noted poet. Henriette was gay and vivacious, and had learned in her uncle's circle to write and speak gracefully. She was thirty when she came to join Mother Barat at Amiens; came, indeed, with such enthusiasm that she refused to stop and see any of the local sights, even the incomparable cathedral, so that the romantic Frenchman who drove her to the convent said to himself: "This young lady must be getting married."

During this time also came two who were to be for many years among Mother Barat's closest associates and most valuable assistants. One was Félicité Desmarquest and the other Catherine de Charbonnel. They could hardly have been more different from each other. Félicité, the daughter of a rich Picardy farmer, was six years younger than Henriette Ducis, but considerably more sedate. She had the usual background. She had sheltered priests and visited prisons, but all this had made her want only to shut out the world and its horrors and become a Carmelite. Like Mother Barat, she gave up the ambition when directed by a priest to go to the new Society instead.

Catherine de Charbonnel was sent by Father Roger. Father Varin saw her only once, and was so unimpressed that he wrote uneasily to Mother Barat, before her perspicacious eye should light on the newcomer, that he was not responsible for choosing her. She arrived at the Rue Neuve in the rain on a worn-out horse. Her clothes were even more worn, she did not look prepossessing, she stammered slightly. Mother Barat was not quite prepared for this. She greeted her kindly but resignedly. The twenty-nine-year-old candidate did not mention her excellent education with the Ursulines, her experience running the finances of her family while the men were fighting the revolutionists, or indeed any of a past almost too varied to have been packed into twenty-nine years.

Cécile Cassini had lately arrived. The two postulants went out for walks with the children, and talkative Cécile soon sized up her shy companion. She found her full of common sense and guessed at her capacity. When Mother Barat offered her scientific postulant a class that was not in science, Cécile got out of it by singing the praises of her companion. Dubious, the Superior made the trial, partly because she had no one else and partly because she had to find out sometime whether her hard-working but unattractive postulant could teach. Fortunately, the doors of the rooms in the Rue Neuve did not close very well, and when the nun in charge of the school for poor children accidentally heard Sister Catherine handling her class like an expert, she was not long in spreading the happy news. The shy little stammerer was soon directing all the studies.

But Mother Barat had other worries than the human material sent to her. Her own health was precarious. The change from outdoor life at Joigny to the almost unrelieved confinement of four years in Paris must have begun the harm. Then, her brother had encouraged her to be as hard on herself as possible, and she had responded only too well. At Amiens, she had very little sleep and not enough to eat. As Superior, she took advantage of her authority to work harder, and eat and sleep less than anyone. She was the despair of Mother Deshayes, the infirmarian. Persuaded to take a small room as her own, so that she would not have to share the common dormitory, she promised herself that now she could stay up, without disturbing the others, and say the prayers she had no time for during the day. Mother Deshayes expected as much, and came to order her to bed. The door had no lock, but the Superior had improvised a crude kind of catch. Mother Deshayes, prevented from exercising her authority on this first night, studied this apparatus, and the next night triumphantly forced her way in and sent her recalcitrant young Superior to bed.

But there were conditions no one could improve. The house was cold and they could not afford heat. There was too much work. Father Varin, appealed to by Mother Deshayes, wrote to urge Mother Barat to take care of herself. She should not try to teach as well as run the house. She might even take a few days of rest, and leave someone else in charge—not, he added, Madame Baudemont. But others were sometimes ill as well as she, and she had no intention of pampering herself.

Shortly before Catherine de Charbonnel's arrival, Claude Capy, the former Poor Clare who had entered with Madame Baudemont, suffered a mental breakdown, seemed to recover, and then relapsed, and the story began malicious gossip that spread rapidly in the small town atmosphere of Amiens. What kind of life were they leading, anyway, if it drove postulants out of their minds? What kind of arrangement was it to have a girl of twenty-four running a community of women with ten times her experience?

It was a pleasant distraction to have Octavie Bailly come back from Rome about this time, bringing with her an Italian nun, Mother Copina. Mother Barat was delighted, and made her companion of the peaceful days in Paris Mistress of Novices, so that she could teach them her own love of prayer to keep them steady in the laborious life they were beginning. But Octavie finally gave in to her desire for Carmel, left Amiens, and lived almost twenty years in the Paris Carmel on the inappropriately named Rue d'Enfer, in the convent where the heroine of Henry James's *The American* took refuge when disappointed in love. Octavie, far from being disappointed, had found her happy ending, and no one envied her more than Sophie Barat.

In March 1804, Mother Barat also had to go to Paris, for the doctors had diagnosed cancer, and the Sisters of Charity there could arrange treatments for her. Mother Deshayes went with her, but came home shortly, leaving her in the care of Sister Marguerite Maillard. Though she stayed in Paris three months, the treatment was evidently unsuccessful, and the time dragged. She wrote home, in some of the earliest of her letters, to lament her situation. Should a nun travel like this, with a full purse and comfort? She went out, she said, as little as she could, and would have liked to give up eating altogether. "I hope," she added, "you are not going to accuse me of being avaricious. But if you want to judge your neighbor rashly, that's your business, not mine. Shall I never, before I die, be given time to shorten my Purgatory? And it will not be only mine! Aren't you afraid of sharing it? But you mean well. God forgive us all!" She was living with a friendly lady who never left her alone. "She has a passion for wanting me to see her family, and it seems as large as Jacob's!" She had little hope of being cured, and was not expecting to live very long—a prospect she faced with no great alarm, and especially with no fear that she might be a loss to the house in Amiens. "Who are we to think God needs us to make His work go on? He can raise up children to Abraham from the stones!"

She was back in Amiens in June, to face a new crisis.

Father Varin had always been uneasy about the union of the Fathers of the Sacred Heart with Paccanari's Fathers of the Faith. He distrusted Paccanari. Others distrusted him even more. He had not even been ordained when he became head of the two united societies. He appeared worldly, ambitious, even a little frivolous. Most of all, he seemed less and less to want to unite with the Jesuits. Among those who distrusted him most was Father John Rozaven, who had been sent to open a house of the Fathers of the Faith in England. Just at the time when Mother Barat was in Paris, Father Varin learned that Rozaven had broken with the Fathers of the Faith and gone to Russia, where he was received by the Superior of the Jesuit remnant there. For Father Varin, the news was a shock. He thought of joining Rozaven, but ecclesiastical authorities in France ad-

vised that the Fathers of the Faith there break with Paccanari
and work as a separate group. The advice seemed good. The
French Fathers elected him their Superior, and broke with
Paccanari.

This move entailed also a break between Mother Barat's
nuns in Amiens and the Diletti in Rome, making the Amiens
house autonomous, under the direction of Mother Barat, with
Father Varin their ecclesiastical superior. However, the link
with Rome had never been close, and there was no reason to
suppose anything would be lost by the new arrangement.

The school in the Rue Neuve, despite occasional difficulties,
was giving full satisfaction to the parents, who were either
nobles or wealthy professional or tradespeople from many
parts of France. The spirit and the studies were excellent. The
nuns followed the example and advice of their neighbors in
the school of the Fathers of the Faith on Rue de l'Oratoire. The
phenomenally gifted Father Loriquet outlined a plan of studies
for them, gave lessons to the nuns, provided them with text-
books he had written on almost every one of the subjects taught,
and even wrote verses to be recited by the pupils on formal
occasions. The scope of the curriculum was impressive, although it stopped short of offering, as did Father Rozaven's
school near "Waux-Hall" in London, "Hebrew and oriental
languages, especially Persian, because of its great usefulness."
It included not only Bible and Church history, French grammar
and language, literature both ancient and modern, mythology,
and the history of the world, but music (singing, harp, piano),
drawing, domestic economy, mathematics and science.

"Domestic economy" included sewing, counting linen, learn-

ing (though not by practice) how to wash various materials
and how to use an iron, helping to purchase food and fuel,
paying bills and counting money, cooking, ordering dinner,
preserving fruits and vegetables, and learning the correct
seasons for planting trees and what trees to prefer. Geography
was studied from "an astronomical, physical, and political point
of view." Practical problems were posed about the position
of stars, and about comparative time in different parts of the
world, but when we read that the pupils recited their scientific
geography in French verse, we can suspect the influence of
Father Loriquet, the elegant poet who had, as a boy, stayed
up much of the night observing the movements of the stars.
Secular masters were imported to teach the young ladies the
accomplishments suited to their state and position in life, but
the nuns carefully surveyed these classes for fear abuses might
be introduced. Great attention was paid to what the French
untranslatably call *maintien,* which is not exactly what used to
be called deportment. Deportment is a vulgar and marginal
affair. *Maintien* reached from minute instructions about how
and when to stand, sit and curtsey, to delicate rules for handling
conversation, greeting, parting and other difficult details of
social intercourse with people of various classes of society, and
could and did, in the right hands, include strong hints about
charity.

One of the characteristics of education in the schools conducted by the Fathers of the Faith, and later by the Jesuits, was
the happy and friendly relationship between teachers and boys.
The poet Lamartine, who attended one of the earliest schools
founded by Father Varin's men, has left a long and loving de-

scription of his memories. A similar relationship existed between
the nuns and their pupils, but the nuns did not have to learn
from Father Loriquet how to establish it. It was the natural
result of their seeing the children as "children of God, redeemed
by the Blood of Jesus Christ and destined to reign eternally
with Him." The words had not yet been written in the Rule, but
Mother Barat, who was to help write them, had such a habit
from the first, and trained her nuns to have it. It followed from
the principle on which her Society was founded: that the glory
of the Heart of Jesus Christ was the whole aim, and that every
work the nuns undertook had that aim in view. They were not
mere school teachers but mothers, bringing children up to
eternal life. Their aim was not to produce learned ladies,
though they sometimes did, but to train Christian mothers.
Father de Tournély, when he foresaw the Society, thought of
it as a way of transforming a country ruined by revolution.
For this, mothers of families must be Christian mothers, strong,
intelligent women rather than mere pious weaklings, women
capable of bringing up their sons as well as their daughters, so
that Frenchmen might again some day see their lives as God-
centered.

When Amiens society discovered that at the Rue Neuve
children were well taught, disciplined and happy, the school
grew. Mother Barat could not take much time from other duties
for the classroom, but she gave the children talks on the love
of God and on their religious duties. She was always serene,
always kind though never weak in her management of the
school, and seemed unaware of her gifts which were so obvious
to others. She preferred to talk with the families of the poor

children, but often wealthy mothers and even more often wealthy fathers were struck by her distinguished manner and the sureness of her tact. She had no ambition to impress them with her knowledge of the world; in fact, she did not, at the time, have much. But she had a quick eye for what made people happy, and she could fit into any situation because of her practical intelligence and her complete lack of self-consciousness. Once she was giving religious instruction to a group of small children who sat close around her. One of them in a moment of distraction, reached into Mother Barat's pocket, took out a small pious book, looked through it, and put it back in the pocket, congratulating herself on having achieved this diversion without attracting the owner's attention. Mother Barat continued calmly until she came to a place where she could confirm what she was teaching by examples. Then she made an impersonal reference to a certain child who, during a lesson, took a book out of a nun's pocket without thinking she had been noticed. As a grandmother, the child of that escapade recalled it, and wondered at the self-control and wisdom of the young teacher.

But the growth of the school itself created a problem, for the house on the Rue Neuve was lamentably small. It did not even have a chapel, and the nuns had to go for Mass on Sunday to the parish church with the children, or on weekdays to the chapel of the Sisters of Notre Dame on the Rue Noyon. Mother Julie Billiart, the remarkable foundress of this congregation, was also a protégée of Father Varin, who wanted a close and loving cooperation between them and Mother Barat's nuns, and who sometimes brought the two groups together to save time by addressing both at once. They shared, as confessor and spiritual director, the attention of a Father of the Faith called Sambucy de St. Estève. Good relations were always maintained with Julie Billiart's daughters, but by 1804 they no longer had to share one chapel.

The Fathers of the Faith had always had difficulties with the authorities of Napoleon, since those cautious gentlemen were concerned about the extensive correspondence carried on by the Fathers, and suspected a plot, and this in spite of the fact that when Napoleon visited Amiens in 1803 he was patriotically tricked into visiting the school on the Rue de l'Oratoire. He had been, in the interests of popularity, making a tour of a factory next door, when someone in the secret led him unsuspectingly through a space in the connecting wall, and he found himself before two hundred boys drawn up in ranks. One boy proceeded to read him a set of fulsome verses by Loriquet, hailing him as a young and valiant hero and comparing him with Caesar, Cyrus and Augustus. Napoleon was impressed by such insight, told the boy to look him up when he graduated, and gave him a job when he did. During 1804, Napoleon issued an order of suppression against the Fathers of the Faith, and though he rescinded the order, they judged it prudent to retire to Montdidier in the suburbs of Amiens. Their house on the Rue de l'Oratoire, a commodious building with a large separate chapel, became available. The crowded school at the Rue Neuve promptly moved in, and the Ladies of Christian Instruction, as Mother Barat's daughters were still called, had a permanent home at last, in the shadow of the largest cathedral in France.

Mother Barat was not to stay in it long. Two months later,

on the twenty-second of November, she set out for Grenoble. It would be two years before she returned, and in the interim, the house would be under the direction of the nun whose influence Father Varin had always opposed, Mother Anne Baudemont.

CHAPTER FOUR

1804–1806

Grenoble

The years that followed were, in spite of trouble and setbacks, among the happiest of Mother Barat's religious life. They brought her two of her dearest companions, and the chance to teach two sets of novices the spirit of the Sacred Heart as she understood it.

For at least a year, there had been talk of a new foundation. In August 1804, Father Varin had written to Amiens about the possibility of a house at Grenoble in Dauphiny. In a few months arrangements had been made, and he had promised that Mother Barat, with some companions, would come to take charge. The house was a huge old Visitation monastery, founded in 1618 by St. Francis de Sales and governed for a time by St. Jane Frances de Chantal. The property was now the possession of a former novice of the house, Rose Philippine Duchesne.

Philippine Duchesne was ten years older than Madeleine Sophie Barat, and in almost everything except her holiness and her intellectual training was completely unlike her. She came of a family much concerned in local and national

politics, and had been educated mostly at home, with her
cousins, the Périer boys, except for two years at the Visitation
Convent of Ste. Marie d'en Haut. At the age of fourteen, she
came home with the intention of returning as a nun. But her
political relatives knew that convents would soon not be safe
places, and her father refused permission. She had, however,
the Duchesne stubbornness, and she entered anyway, simply
going up the hill one day for a visit to the monastery, and sending back word that she was staying. A kind of truce ensued.
Her father allowed her to stay but would not consent to her
making vows, and she was still a novice four years later when
the community were dispersed, as her father had foreseen,
by the Revolution. There followed the usual years of clandes-
tine service to priests.

When life quieted, Philippine's first thought was to return to
religious life at the Visitation. The convent on the hill had been
used as a prison, and was in an advanced state of dilapidation.
The community were by now mostly old ladies broken down by
suffering, and though Philippine had the property turned over
to her through the good offices of her always useful relatives,
she could not persuade her former sisters to return, except for
one brief and unsuccessful trial. Almost in despair, she opened
the house to religious of other dispersed communities, and tried
to begin a school. This also failed. Early in 1804, there were in
the great, half-ruined house only four religious, including
herself, and a handful of pupils. Then, the brother of one of the
nuns, Father Rivet, vicar general of Grenoble, told her about
the new Society dedicated to the Sacred Heart, and put her
in touch with the Fathers of the Faith in Lyons.

On the feast of St. Ignatius, July 31, Father Rivet came to

visit Ste. Marie, bringing with him Father Varin and Father Roger. They went through the house, expressing great satisfaction with the chapel of the Sacred Heart, but refusing to commit themselves in any way. They talked a good deal about the necessity of going slowly and thinking things over, until Philippine, whose chief virtue was not, then or ever, patience, inquired subacidly what Francis Xavier would have accomplished if he had followed such advice. The priests enjoyed the remark, but still temporized, until just before leaving, Father Varin said he would send Mother Barat to look things over.

It was on such an errand, to find the "great and generous soul" Father Varin had promised her, that Sophie Barat set out in the worst season of the year for a journey of over three hundred miles to the southeast. Her companions were Mother Rosalie Debrosse, who had made her vows with Mother de Charbonnel the day before the departure, and faithful Sister Marguerite Maillard. The journey was made by those public coaches in which Mother Barat was to spend such a great part of her long life. There were several stop-offs, one of two days in Paris, where an encouraging letter from Father Varin awaited her, and where preparations were being made for Napoleon's coronation; another of a week at Joigny, to visit her relatives and offer to take into her school some of the girls in her sister's rapidly increasing family. Several of these girls eventually entered her Society. A third stop was made in Lyons, where Father Varin wanted her to see postulants.

Another letter from Father Varin came to her there, assuring her everything was getting on well in Amiens, and remarking that if you wanted to win souls for God you had to have a great

soul yourself; that Xavier could not have set out to convert the
universe if he had not had a soul larger than the universe.
Sophie Barat never thought of herself as a great soul. She said
sixty years later that she had been sent to Grenoble because
she was the one member the Amiens community could get
along without. However, she had promised to be ready for
whatever God might plan, and never to be astonished at how
great or how hard His plans might seem.

As she came into Grenoble in the cold late afternoon of the
thirteenth of December, the city itself must have seemed, to
the eyes of a girl brought up in the valley of the Yonne, a
symbol of how great those plans might be. The slopes of Joigny
would have been swallowed up here, where Grenoble, at the
junction of the Isère and the Drac, looked up at its ring of
snowy peaks that "batter the vision with successive grandeurs."
The city itself is in a valley so deep that mountain peaks loom
at the end of every street. But the monastery high above looks
down at the city spread out at its feet, and up at the white
immensities of the Alps. Mother Barat had never in her life
seen a cloistered convent, and her vivid imagination quickened
at the thought of the saints who had lived in the dark mass of
buildings toward which she was climbing, and at the happier
thought that she might revive the worship of the Sacred Heart
in a house belonging to the sisters of Margaret Mary Alacoque.

After the driver of the coach had been paid, there were still
steps to climb. The three tired women, not knowing what to
expect, entered a low, narrow, damp corridor, but before they
had time to be bewildered, Philippine Duchesne came rushing
to meet them, threw herself on her knees before this startled girl
ten years her junior, and kissed her feet, crying out: "Blessed on

the mountains are the feet of those who bring good tidings of peace!" From then on, Mother Barat knew what she was to expect, from Philippine Duchesne at least, and in spite of what lay ahead of her in the coming months, her heart lifted with relief at the sight of such faith and humility.

Sophie Barat, as Philippine Duchesne that day saw her for the first time, was small, rather dark-complexioned, and not very impressive, certainly not beautiful; but her look was alert and her glance quick and her smile kindly. Her high forehead and prominent chin and cheek bones added decisiveness and energy to her expression. Her walk and all her movements were swift, though controlled, and she spoke with such vivacity that her eyes brightened and color rose in her cheeks. Her obvious though apparently easy holding under of naturally impetuous reactions conveyed a sense of power.

There were five in the community, including Emilie Giraud, who was little more than a child, and whom Mother Barat trained to be one of her best superiors; and Marie Balastron, the excitable "chère Balastron" of many letters to come, whose favorite exclamation was Father Varin's "How good God is!" of which she made a verse with "Que Dieu est bon" rhyming with Balastron. Mother Barat at once set about the work of changing this motley group into Religious of the Sacred Heart. She took her time about it, however. Father Roger was supposed to have given a retreat to start the process, but she knew Father Roger and persuaded him to decide that the retreat had better be put off. He was a fiery, impetuous man who, when he was made master of Jesuit novices some years later, proved too vigorous even for them. He could be, one of his brothers reported, rather rough, and talked a little too consistently about victories over oneself and violence to be done to oneself, and he worked especially at breaking the self-will of his young men. Mother Barat did not think such an introduction appropriate, especially for timid Emilie, for Balastron whose imagination multiplied everything, and for Philippine herself, whose natural tendency to Father Roger's methods was already over-developed.

It was Advent, and one of Sophie Barat's special devotions was to the Child of Bethlehem. Father Varin had told her to be firm when necessary, hard never, gentle always and everywhere. There would, soon enough, be traditions from the past to be given up, patience and calm to be learned, studies to be labored at. For the time being, she did not mention these, but only the God Who so loved men as to send them His only Son, and that Son's taking the form of a child helpless enough to arouse anyone's chivalry.

Christmas was bitterly cold in the empty, echoing monastery, where doors and windows had been broken, and snow poured in unchecked. The chapel itself was lacking three windows and a door, but it was a superb chapel nevertheless, with its rich altars, its gilding, its walls and vaulted ceiling covered with paintings, and its wooden grill, which reminded Mother Barat that she would have to tell Philippine that Religious of the Sacred Heart, unlike Visitation nuns, did not have grills. The cloister garden with its cross was deep in snow, and they all felt close to the young mother who had warmed her Child in her arms eighteen hundred years before on a hill in Judea. "The cold was intense," Philippine noted, "but we did not feel it." It did not occur to her that although she did not feel it others might. Mother Barat thought first of others. It was a habit she tried to teach her new daughter.

What she began to teach them all, once the holidays were over and their regular novitiate began, was what she went on teaching all her life: that God loved them and had, as a Man, died for them, and that in return they must give Him that consistent love which turns into sanctity. The word "love," which occurred so often on her lips and under her pen, is a dangerous word, and may easily strike some as sentimental. What did she mean by it? Love, for her as for all saints, was a spiritual act by which you allowed God to take hold of you and change you. Why did you have to be changed?—because you were so made that happiness could come only from giving yourself completely to God, but you inherited, against God's original intentions, a flaw that made you cling instead to your autonomy. Unless you gave up this clinging to yourself, you could not be happy. But more than that, God, in His plan for reshaping men who had deformed themselves, so arranged matters that men must help one another. They must help one another as the Son of God, in His life on earth, had helped them; that is, by prayer, suffering, and direct apostolic action.

A few men and women choose deliberately a form of life given over to making others (as well as themselves) happy in the only way they can really *be* happy. Some, like the Carmelites Sophie Barat so envied, use mostly the first and second method, praying, as Christ prayed in His long nights on the hills of Judea and Galilee, and suffering as He suffered on Calvary. Others, while not neglecting the first and second methods, devote themselves mostly to the third, teaching what life means and where happiness is to be found, or merely going about doing good, so that men may see love in action and believe in it, and in their turn give themselves to God to be changed.

But many see a touch of morbidity in the stress on suffering, and on "killing," as the word mortification implies, something in yourself. There is only one way round this difficulty, a way few people are willing to take. It is to follow the terse direction: "taste and see." The quotation ends: "that the Lord is sweet." But it might end: "that this way of killing things in yourself is also sweet," though not sweet in itself, for it is not a perversion which revels in pain for its own sake. Nineteenth-century rhetoric, from which Mother Barat's own style and even more the style of Philippine Duchesne were not free, may give the impression that they find suffering sweet in itself. They did not ever mean this. What they meant is that there is a joy which can coexist with suffering, although it takes away no natural repugnance to it. This joy has been defined as the inner strength that enables one to surmount repugnance. To vary another Gospel figure: it is the joy a woman can feel even when she is in labor, because she looks forward to a child that is to be born.

What Madeleine Sophie Barat taught her ill-assorted little group at Grenoble was that a Religious of the Sacred Heart must give herself entirely to this sort of motherhood, not only for the happiness of her spiritual children, but far more for the Son of God, Who will be glorified by a wilful choosing to share in His work of Love.

When she had taught them this doctrine and exercised them gently in practising it, she felt they were ready for the thunders of Father Roger, who played the same melody, but *fortissimo*. The climax of his retreat was an order that, on the last day, each one give up to Mother Barat whatever she most clung to. No one brought anything. At the end of the day, Father Roger, understandably frustrated by this failure of his efforts, asked why he had not been obeyed. Mother Duchesne retorted that she could not very well bring to her new Superior the house and the people in it, but that she clung to nothing else. She would, eventually, cling not even to them.

It was, then, a good beginning, and things went on well. It is interesting to compare a letter of Mother Barat's written to Mother Duchesne in November 1804, with another from Lyons five months later. The first addresses her as Madame, and is gracious but formal, as only a French letter, full of the *convenances,* can be formal. In the second, Philippine is her dear daughter, and she teases her about her faults in a way only intimate affection could allow, discusses the "death to self," to which Philippine so aspired, in poetic variations on the Canticle of Canticles, and ends with a longing to have news of what is happening on the Mountain.

Almost thirty years later, she wrote to Mother Duchesne, then on the missions in Missouri, that letters from America woke memories of hours spent with her on the calm, lonely mountain in Dauphiny. She contrasted these hours with her life in Paris, in the middle of the chaos of business and of grandeurs which she avoided as much as she could. She distracted herself from all this, she went on to say, by envying Philippine her vast forests on the shores of the Mississippi, where, as a matter of fact, Philippine was then in the even more chaotic whirlpool of American business crises, bills to be paid with no money, and young Americans to be civilized. In 1804, in the battered monastery on the edge of the Alps, the two saints had a brief honeymoon of religious life to which they looked back nostalgically all their lives, without ever doubting that it was better to give it up.

There were, even then, troubles enough, many of them coming from gossip in the town, where the Duchesnes were well-known. Although the children in the school were happy and charmed by Mother Barat, comments over coffee cups in the city below ran on how disgracefully young was the new Superior, and how incompetent the teaching. And why were they cutting down so on visitors from the outside? Possible postulants were discouraged by the gossip. Mother Barat met it by the method she taught her novices. Even while she was restraining Philippine from being too hard on herself, she received letters from Father Varin like one which came in February, 1805: "Your courageous decision to fast this Lent made your brother, who was present when I received your letter, shrug his shoulders. I really cannot understand you. . . . If there is not the authority of a doctor to prevent you, there is the authority of the natural law, the law of God and the law of the Church which 1) forbids you to commit suicide, and 2) orders you to take the means necessary to carry out the duties of your state in life." He was not unaware, however, that, shrug his shoulders as he might, it was Louis Barat who had started his sister on this road. He said to him, when he learned that Madeleine Sophie was ill: "You are the one who ruined her health." Father Barat, who had learned gentleness from Joseph Varin, admitted it was true, but both knew that it would not be easy, even if it proved possible, to persuade Sophie to change the road on which her brother had set her.

In the first year there were visits from several of the Fathers of the Faith, especially Father Roger, Father Barat, and Father Varin himself. Only a few months after Mother Barat's own arrival at Grenoble, Geneviève Deshayes came to join the community, and very shortly, Henriette Grosier was called to take charge of a foundation at Belley which soon fell through. This meant that the two first companions of Mother Barat, who best understood what the Society of the Sacred Heart was meant to be, were withdrawn from Amiens, and that Anne Baudemont was left to make of it what she liked. Meanwhile, it became necessary, before allowing the novices in Dauphiny to make vows, to put on paper for the Bishop of Grenoble some statement of the Society's aims and methods. Fathers Roger and Varin worked at this document, which was presented with an introduction by Mothers Barat and Duchesne.

As set down by Joseph Varin, who had the plans of Léonor de Tournély to protect, this was the outline: the aim was to work, with the help of God, for the perfection of the members of the Society and for the salvation of others, by a pure intention of giving glory only to God, by entire detachment from the world and from self, by zeal and gentleness towards others, and by obedience to superiors. After a summary of the spiritual exercises of the community, and of their work in boarding and free schools, a final section described the simplicity and poverty of their life, its lack of extraordinary mortifications, its insistence on prayer. The houses would be cloistered, it said, and there would be a Superior General.

The Bishop approved. On November 21, a little less than a year after Mother Barat had come to Grenoble, Mother Duchesne made her vows, with Mother Rivet, Emilie Giraud, and another new arrival, Henriette Girard. Henriette, a woman of over forty, had been puzzled, when she first came, because everyone talked of "crosses," and she could not see that anyone was noticeably suffering. Mother Deshayes had explained that their cross was not to be able to love God or to make others love Him as He deserved to be loved. A cross of another kind was in store both for them and for Mother Barat. A week after the ceremony, Father Varin announced that she would leave for Amiens at once for the election of the Superior General mentioned in the summary presented to the Bishop. She would leave Mother Deshayes at Grenoble as superior.

She arrived at Amiens on December 14. Exteriorly, everything was in order. The regulations were carefully followed. The nuns were serving God fervently. Fathers Varin and Roger spoke to the community about the hope of soon taking openly the name of Society of the Sacred Heart, and a seal was adopted which carried the image of the Sacred Heart. The Bishop of Amiens approved the summary worked out in Grenoble, and on January 18, the community came together to vote for the Superior General. Father Varin presided. Father Roger assisted. The confessor of the house, Father Sambucy de St. Estève, was allowed to be present as a witness. The nuns in the other houses who had made their vows sent their vote in writing. Mother Barat was elected Superior General, but by only one vote.

She spent no more than five months at Amiens, for the house was no longer hers; not that she would ever have thought of it in such terms, but we can, meaning that it no longer followed the spirit she had learned from Father Varin and he had learned from de Tournély. The house was Mother Baudemont's, and her ways were good; but they were not the ways of the Society as Mother Barat had been taught to understand them. Father Varin's letters to this ex-Poor Clare, after he had reluctantly allowed her to become Superior, had urged her to show charity and deference to others, and not to take a tone of command, as, he reminded her, she often did. "Learn of Me, that I am meek and humble of heart," was the watchword of a superior in the Sacred Heart manner. He had never had to make such suggestions to Sophie Barat. But more dangerous than Mother Baudemont's tendency to dominate others was her equally strong tendency to allow anyone she trusted to dominate her. She had absolute trust in the confessor, St. Estève, whom Mother Deshayes described as a man of letters with a brilliant imagination, but of the climbing variety. He was a genius, she admitted, but a restless, change-loving one. He and Mother Baudemont mutually supported each other, and neither paid much attention to Sophie Barat, a young religious of twenty-six, with almost no experience, and certainly, they must have thought, with no spirit.

Mother Barat had no desire to dispute their authority. When she came back to Amiens, it was in the firm expectation of seeing someone else elected Superior General. In the month's interval before the voting, she had talked a good deal about being a mere barrel-maker's daughter from a small town; and when her nephew, Louis Dussaussoy, came to Amiens to study at the school of the Fathers of the Faith, she took care to put him, in his badly cut country clothes, very much in evidence. The

situation in Amiens, which she only too well understood, made
her election as Superior General a greater blow than it would
otherwise have been. But she did not wail over it, nor did she
go about speaking ill of herself; she simply kept quiet and
hoped people would see for themselves how ineffective she
was. Two days later she was able to write a gay letter to Mother
Duchesne in which she hardly mentioned the election.

Father Varin had hoped that, after the voting, they might
go on to draw up detailed rules for the Society. But once dis-
cussions began, it was evident that he and St. Estève did not
see eye to eye, and he decided it was better to let the affair
work out with time. He merely said that now, with a Superior
General of its own, the Society had no need of his official services, and he left Amiens—to Mother Barat, presumably, but
really to Mother Baudemont and the confessor.

Mother Barat spent more time with the school than with the
community. She was distressed to notice that the same children
she had known a year before as simple, pious, and happy in
their school life, were now passionately interested in worldly
pleasure, so that it was not the love but the fear of God one
had to preach to them. She was never averse to preaching the
fear of God, but always, with her, it was a prelude to preaching
the love of God. She found herself remembering and regretting
the Grenoble children, especially Euphrosine Jouve, Mother
Duchesne's niece, wilful and naughty, but with the straightness
of the Duchesnes, and their capacity for positive action, and
for courageously acknowledging and repairing that action if
they later discovered it was wrong. Euphrosine, her aunt foresaw, might be a religious some day, and she was brought up

with that possibility in view, but that did not mean she was kept in a hothouse. She was merely taught to consider the value of her actions and to fight against the passion for pleasure, as these frothy sprigs at Amiens could not do.

CHAPTER FIVE

1806–1808

Poitiers

Mother Barat felt useless at Amiens, and wrote to Mother Duchesne after only three months there that she was longing to be back on "her mountain." Mother Duchesne had been sending her ecstatic letters about an offer she had just received to go on the American missions, and Mother Barat answered that she had the same ambition. She arrived at Grenoble on the twentieth of May, but a few weeks later Father Varin wrote suggesting a foundation in Poitiers, clear across the country.

The request interrupted her attempt to make the studies at Grenoble conform to Father Loriquet's outline and the developments of that outline worked out by Mother de Charbonnel. Leaving Mother Duchesne to carry on this work, often during the hours when she should have been asleep, the new Superior General prepared for another journey. To Father Varin, she wrote her fear of being an obstacle to the work in Poitiers. He replied that he did not see why she took such pleasure in perpetually trembling. She should realize that the faultier the material used, the more hope there was that the work would be His. By the tenth of July, after only six weeks

in Grenoble, she set out for Poitiers with Henriette Girard,
partly because Henriette was a woman of considerably more
age and experience than herself, partly perhaps because Poitiers was less than a hundred and fifty miles from the Bordeaux
diocese of Archbishop d'Aviau, whom the Girards had sheltered
during the Revolution.

This is the first of Mother Barat's journeys of which we have
a detailed account. She had been unwell before leaving Grenoble, suffering from a recurrence of the cancer unsuccessfully
treated in Paris two years earlier. After a two-day stop in Lyons,
where she found herself much worse, she and Mother Girard
set out again, and Mother Barat, as she wrote to Mother Duchesne, "complained mildly to Our Lord," pointing out how
disagreeable it would be if she were to become ill in such company as a public coach provided. Having prayed, she stopped
worrying, and just after they had passed the town limits, she
found herself suddenly and completely cured. She had done
nothing, she insists, to improve her condition, and the heat and
weariness were more than enough to make her much worse,
even without the dirty inns where they had been staying and
the bad food they had been served there. Nevertheless, she re-
peats, "I am completely cured." And there was no sign of the
disease thereafter.

This was a promising beginning. The coach to Moulins,
about a hundred miles northwest of Lyons, had other passengers, all men, who teased the two nuns jovially, and disturbed them by their frivolous talk. Mother Barat, as she told
the Grenoble community in her letter, sat wondering why God
had saved her, of all people, from living on the same level of
triviality. When the coach stopped near farms, she made friends

with the children, tried to find out how much catechism they knew, invariably found they knew next to nothing, and wished urgently that she could stay and repair these simple deficiencies instead of trying to rule a Society only half of whom wanted her (the half who did *not* want her, she no doubt thought, being the wiser).

When they reached Moulins, they discovered no coach was setting out for Limoges, their next stop. Finally, they heard the mail coach would be going there forty-eight hours later, but the driver was not anxious to take them on because he would have to give them the only good seats. Not too hopeful, they went to church early on the second day. Mother Barat, however, felt herself urged to leave almost at once. She found the man had changed his mind, but had not been able to find them, and was on the verge of leaving without them. She tore Mother Girard from her prayers, and they were soon on the road again, being entertained by their sixty-year-old driver, a man who had abandoned good prospects in the world for the excitement of driving in all weather, day and night, along bad roads, and who drove with a recklessness appropriate to his adventurous dis-position. There was every chance that they might end their career in one of the ditches over which their driver urged his horses. The nuns tried to counsel a little caution, but their sporting driver was deaf to suggestion. However, his age was against him, and presently he found himself feeling ill. Mother Barat pressed on him a little cordial which the sisters at Gre-noble had given her for emergencies. He replied austerely that he never drank, but did not persevere long in his refusal. They gave him only a small amount, but he promptly fell asleep, leaving the horses, which were probably more reliable than he was, to get on alone.

At Limoges, there was still no public coach to be had for the last lap before Poitiers. A priest to whom they had been recommended suggested that they hire a private vehicle. A driver turned up at the inn and the priest guaranteed his respectability. The nuns haggled prudently over the price, stressing that they were to stop off in Bellac at ten for Mass next day, which was Sunday. The driver promised, and said the trip would take four days in all. So far they had not seen the offered coach. When it was too late to withdraw, they discovered that it was a kind of freight cart, piled high with stuff. In front the owner had rigged up a crazy structure of hoops and canvas, within the doubtful shelter of which he proposed to establish them on some hay and their own bags. Mother Barat thought such a poor, humble way of coming into Poitiers would probably draw the favor of God on her new foundation. Mother Girard had not sufficiently advanced in humility to share this point of view. To spare her feelings, they arranged to mount their vehicle only outside town, where they would not have the crowd to watch them. When they did try to get up, it was extraordinarily difficult, and the driver, who was named Cadence, had to haul and shove mightily before his passengers were aboard.

After lumbering along slowly for hours, they came to an isolated inn and put up there for the night, with what Mother Barat called a "university of rats holding their assembly," and making them think the place had been attacked by robbers. At the end of the third day, the cart broke down, and Cadence said it would take four hours to mend it. Since next day, July

22, was the feast of St. Mary Magdalen, her patron saint, Mother Barat was glad of the chance to go to confession and communion, of which they had been deprived since leaving Lyons. Next day they started off early, in pouring rain. The distance to Poitiers was short, but the rain grew steadily worse. They rumbled into town in a bedraggled state, conscious of watching eyes behind every window they passed, and were set down in a yard where the freight was to be unloaded.

Complete strangers in Poitiers, the two nuns had to find a kind-hearted woman to take them and their bags to the house where they were vaguely expected. It was still raining, they were soaked to the skin, and neither had much hope of their being recognized, on arrival, as religious come to make a foundation.

The house they had been offered was a monastery built in 1618 for monks of a branch of the Cistercian order, called Feuillants. About the time of the Revolution it had been bought by three sisters named Chobelet, who tried to begin a school and gather teachers to form a religious congregation. They had not succeeded, and Mademoiselle Lydia Chobelet, the only sister still connected with the project, had lost hope and already sold the property. When Father Lambert told her about the religious in Amiens and in Grenoble, they managed to buy back the house.

Mademoiselle Chobelet was a woman in her forties, and had one companion, Josephine Bigeu, more than ten years younger. Like Mother Duchesne, Josephine had had a boy's education, but she was thoroughly feminine. As a girl, she had tried desperate expedients to change the color of her hair from its unfashionable red—a trick which would have made Mother

Duchesne indignant. She had the miraculous combination of holiness, intelligence and charm so useful to a new teaching order. Mother Barat, being greeted reservedly by her that damp day in the vast, empty parlor of the old Feuillants monastery, would have been cheered had she been able to foresee her future. For the moment, after the long wait in the silent room, she could only note that her two hostesses welcomed her civilly, but had obviously not been given time to look forward to meeting her, and so were not enthusiastic. Looking about the room, which had only the barest sticks of furniture, for everything had been sold in preparation for departure, Mother Barat found this poverty an even better augury for God's work than the rescue of the house itself.

Next morning, things looked brighter. She met the two remaining pupils and the two servants, and presented the statutes of her Society to the vicar general of the diocese, who soon approved them. She presented them also to the two ladies at the Feuillants, but did not try to influence their decision. As soon as ecclesiastical approval came, they accepted it as the will of God. The always interested neighbors, who had been watching the Chobelet sisters struggling with their enterprise for years, said frankly that Lydia was a fool to give up her independence to this unknown young woman; but Lydia and Josephine were not bothered by gossip. Everything was turned over to Mother Barat, and her hostesses became her obedient daughters.

Not all of the local reaction had been unfavorable. Young girls in the neighborhood who wanted to be nuns showed up asking to join her. She talked with them all individually. Most had problems. For the moment, she accepted none, for she

wished to go on to Bordeaux, where another Father of the
Faith, Father Enfantin, had interested young ladies to introduce to her. Father Enfantin, one of the most engaging of
Father Varin's companions, was always getting himself into
tight situations. He was not a brilliant student or a good
preacher, and he had not much natural prudence, but he was
holy and humble, and so usually muddled through with excellent results. This time, he had stirred up a pious hornets' nest.

During a mission he and Father Lambert gave in Bordeaux,
some young women with aspirations to the religious life had
formed themselves into a choir for the services. Encouraged by
this community project, and much discouraged by their relatives whenever they suggested becoming nuns, they thought
out an original scheme. One of them, an orphan, had a vineyard outside the city, with a small house—no more than a
barn—attached. One evening, after the last instruction of the
day, six of them walked together to the vineyard and made a
convent out of the barn by settling down for the night. None of
them being especially practical, they had not brought any
food, but there was some straw, and they lay down, hungry,
but no doubt feeling all the more virtuous for that, and slept
the sleep of the triumphant. Meanwhile, their loving families
were frantic. Happily, an old governess of one girl had been
let in on the secret. She calmed the weeping mothers and
angry fathers, and persuaded them not to go, as they were
fully prepared to do, and drag their recalcitrant daughters
home by main force. Leave them alone, she urged. They were
young and had good appetites and nothing to eat. The result
would be inevitable.

Next morning, still hungry, they came to church. Word of

their escapade had spread in the parish, and they were greeted
with hoots by the younger set, and with frowns by the sober.
Unmoved they went back adamantly to their barn. Their anxious mothers, thinking little of the starving-out strategy, sur-
reptitiously supplied them food, and this arrangement might
have gone on indefinitely had it not been pointed out to the
solitaries that they were making fools not only of themselves
but of religion, and especially of the Fathers who were giving
the mission, and who were, of course, being cursed by the
irate fathers, and by other fathers who feared their daughters
might show just as little sense—not because they were particularly holy, but because the whole thing was so romantic. As a
matter of fact, even Father Enfantin had had sense enough to
keep absolutely aloof from the affair, but since the priests were
blamed anyway, he got leave to gather the girls temporarily
in a convent of nuns called Les Dames Vincent. There he talked
to them about Mother Barat's nuns, and explained their rules.
They liked what they heard, and promptly determined to live
in the house with the nuns, but as a separate group, and to
follow the rules of the Sacred Heart, with one of them, Elizabeth Maillucheau, as Superior.

Father Enfantin's plan was that a house of the Society should
be opened in Bordeaux, for he had promised the partly pacified
parents that their daughters would not leave the city. Mother
Barat saw the young ladies, now respectably housed with Les
Dames Vincent, and saw under the not-very-sensible exterior,
signs of true vocation to the religious life. She would accept all
six. More than thirty other women asked to join her. She saw
them all kindly. Most she advised to join other orders, and suggested orders they might join. Some she put off for the time

being. Of the thirty or more, she accepted only two. In the intervals, she was taken about Bordeaux to inspect possible convents, and did not protest, since she had been told that Archbishop d'Aviau wanted a foundation. After a week, during which no suitable site was found, Mother Barat went to the Archbishop and told him that, to her deep regret, they were not yet worthy to establish themselves in his diocese, but would try to become so. The Archbishop, as a courtly French-man, could do no less than give her his blessing, and say he would be glad to lend her these eight lambs from his flock pro-vided he had her promise that they should be returned eventu-ally to the home fold. She gave no promise but said she hoped this might happen.

Then, anxious about her two new daughters waiting in Poi-tiers to begin their novitiate, she hurried to make arrangements so that she and Mother Girard, whose presence had probably helped to make things smooth with the Archbishop, might go on to the Feuillants as soon as possible. The postulants were divided into groups, lest their departure en masse cause too much stir. Mother Barat kept Elizabeth Maillucheau with her, and spent two days calling on the parents of her postulants. All were impressed by her, and the fact that she had been will-ing to accept their daughters made them think better of the whole business. They ended by being proud to be associated with so gracious, efficient and palpably holy a young foundress. All this visiting made her the last to arrive at the Feuillants. Getting out of the coach, she slipped and hurt her foot pain-fully, so that she had to stop at a friend's house for first aid before she could walk to the convent. She found the new-comers who had preceded her already very much at home and glad to see her. It was the sixth of September 1806. She decided that on the eighth, feast of the Nativity of the Blessed Virgin, the novitiate would officially begin.

There could hardly have been a better place for it. Isolated and silent, surrounded by spacious grounds and further on by a ring of hills, the house with its great vaulted rooms and its memories of past holiness lent itself perfectly to an atmosphere of prayer and dedication. To the ten postulants was added an eleventh, Mademoiselle de Chastaignier. Of this group, several were to give memorable service to the Society they had just joined, and pass down to the next generation the spirit of love and sacrifice they had learned in the quiet, monotonous days of this first of the Society's novitiates. They studied, prayed, worked together, cleaned the house, and loved one another. Josephine Bigeu continued to manage the tiny school, with Mother Girard to second her. Very soon Sister Josephine was also helping to direct the activities of the other novices.

Elizabeth Maillucheau, the leading spirit of the Bordeaux group, was allowed to change her name to Thérèse, in honor of the reformer of Carmel, and her eagerness to do so reveals what she was. She became the mystic, as the popular word describes it, of the young Society, showered all her life with extraordinary gifts of prayer. Mother Barat loved her specially, and in the last years of her life envied her opportunity to devote herself more and more exclusively to contemplation. In the beginnings, she saw to it that she had very little time for it, partly to test the genuineness of her attraction, partly to give her the chance for sacrifice which is the proper food of sanctity, and partly to train her for active service. She was not exactly learned, but knew languages, including a little Latin, wrote verses, composed airs, and played the harp—all useful if minor accomplishments. But no one ever succeeded in making her practical. She did not become a tireless apostle like Mother Duchesne, or a great teacher like Mother Bigeu, or an efficient organizer of new foundations like Mother de Charbonnel, or a first-rate Mistress of Novices like Mother Desmarquest. Her part in the organization was prayer. When she turned her hand to anything else, disaster too often dogged her. She prayed, and (perhaps therefore) the others succeeded. But at Poitiers, Mother Barat kept turning her out of the chapel to cut hay for the donkey.

The most important work of the novices was to learn the ways of God and to understand themselves so that they could set themselves firmly in God's ways. Many distinguished priests came to preach to them and to teach them. Twice a week, Mother Barat spoke to them of the life of Christ and of the rules of the Society. Her speech, then and always, was a kind of pastiche of quotations from the Gospels and from St. Paul. She had favorites, which recur in all her letters and other writings: "Who shall separate us from the love of Christ? My life is hidden with Christ. I live, now not I, but Christ lives in me. I can do all things in Him Who strengthens me." She wanted, and she made her novices want, to inflame the world with the love of Christ.

Love, as she understood it, meant denying yourself, so as to become what God intended you to be. God intended you to be like Christ. The more like Him you were, the more you were yourself, but perhaps not the self you were accustomed to. To be like Christ was to serve others. "I came not to be ministered unto," Christ had said, "but to minister." Mother

Barat, to give her novices the chance to practise what they were learning, did not try to lessen the hardships of their life in this deserted, partially ruined old house. They spent hours in hard work, even carrying stones to help with the building repairs. The Superior was with them at every chore, never losing her dignity or her kindness. To hard work was added poverty. There were only five pupils. None of the novices had dowries. They kept alive only because Sister Chobelet's maid, Marie, knew the shifts of the real poor, picking up a few vegetables overlooked at the regular picking, selling things for a few cents that looked to everyone else not worth a single cent, using her credit with the tradespeople. The nuns' clothing was mended and patched until nothing of the original was left. Sister Chastaignier, an active woman, used to managing the lives of the miserable, was in despair, sometimes, as she looked at herself and wondered what she was accomplishing.

She learned, a little more slowly than some of the others, that Mother Barat intended to disabuse them of the illusion that they were doing or could do anything indispensable. After all, if you believe that there is a God Who is almighty then you cannot think He needs your work. He can, presumably, do in the twinkling of an eye what you labor at. But if you also believe in a God Who became Man because He loved men, then you must be convinced that He wants *you*. The difficulty is to know when you are really giving yourself to Him. The solution, generally, is that if you do what you have good reason to believe He had ordered, then you are giving yourself to Him through your most intimate faculty, your will. Religious life is a way of assuring yourself that you are constantly doing the

Will of God in the smallest detail, therefore constantly giving yourself to Him.

But the God to Whom you gave yourself was not a vague Providence or a stern lawgiver, and the way of obeying was not one you had to work out blindly for yourself. Christ was the Way, and Christ was God. The method Mother Barat taught was the method St. Paul taught: conformity with Christ. To want what He wanted, to think as He thought, to act as He had acted—this was the secret. To know Christ and Him crucified —this was the science. And "crucifixion" was too exalted a word, certainly, for the small daily deaths obedience demanded. But you practised this preliminary daily dying cheerfully, in the hope that something harder might eventually be asked.

We have no proof that Mother Barat yet knew what God's plans were for her Society. She contented herself with fashioning supple instruments He could use when His moment came, as He was now, after a mysterious preparation, using her. If Thérèse MailLucheau, instead of praying in the chapel, went to watch the cows, she was not separating herself from God but giving herself to Him more closely. Almost a century and a quarter later, Christ was to appear to a novice, Josefa Menendez, in these same cloisters at Poitiers and ask her where she was coming from and where she was going. She said she was coming from the chapel and going to close the windows. He taught her to say instead that she was coming from Love and going to Love, because everything she did was done through obedience for Him.

These are notions easier to talk about than to act on. In those months at the Feuillants, to which all the novices who had shared them looked back for a lifetime with joy, they were learning to practise these things laboriously, so that they might later do them almost by instinct.

Not all the novices at Poitiers were learning for the first time. When Mother Barat had first come to Poitiers, a local priest had suggested to her as a postulant Suzanne Geoffroy, who was then such a subject of dispute among the clergy of the area that it seemed unwise to admit her. Mother Barat, however, liked what she had heard, and kept this unusual candidate in mind. She was already forty-six years old, had never responded to efforts to educate her, and never learned to spell; but she had a brilliant wit, and a magnetic attraction for others, which had nothing to do with beauty, for that she did not possess. She knew very young that she was meant to be a nun, but told herself that though it was all very well to die a nun, she could not face *living* as a nun.

At twenty-one, she had a mysterious experience of union with Christ, which persisted even when she tried to distract herself by her social life. In a moment of fervor, she tried to become a Carmelite, but the prioress told her she was meant to save her soul by saving others, a diagnosis supported by an old ex-Jesuit who told her that she would become a nun in a Society whose foundress was still, when he spoke, playing with her dolls. It was 1787. Suzanne was twenty-six and Sophie Barat eight. He also told her this Society would be consecrated to the Sacred Heart and would combine the spirit of St. Teresa with that of St. Ignatius. The Revolution completed the work of her conversion. Afterward she tried to organize works of various kinds and founded two religious congregations, but could never attach herself permanently to any, for she believed the old priest's prediction. This vacillation annoyed the clergy, and she was even preached against in public. Once when this happened at a meeting of charitable ladies, she disconcerted the priest by going to him afterward and saying: "I see God has given you great insight into my soul. Will you be kind enough to hear my confession?" He was soon one enemy struck off her list.

Less than a year after the foundation at Poitiers, Mother Barat was asked to open a house in Niort, slightly southwest of Poitiers. She said she had no one who could be the Superior of such a foundation, but that if they did not mind having Suzanne Geoffroy, she would train her and send her. Suzanne entered at Poitiers in October 1807. She was to live to be eighty-four, spending her years as Superior at Niort and Bordeaux, but when she joined the novitiate, she was already a mistress of the spiritual life, especially of the doctrine that you give nothing to God so long as you do not give Him yourself.

Thérèse Maillucheau and Josephine Bigeu had been allowed to take vows, after only six months' training. In April 1807, Mother Barat went to Paris to consult Father Varin about more suggested foundations. During her absence, she put Thérèse in charge of the house and appointed Josephine to assist her. She was away less than a month, and the joy at her return she herself describes. She arrived during evening recreation, and after much embracing all proceeded to the chapel. Her intention was simply to present herself to the Master of the house, but her daughters had other views. Thérèse intoned the *Te Deum*, for the double joy of seeing her Superior and being relieved of authority, and the others took up the triumphal chant.

The startled Superior rose to stop them, but they were in full career, and she resigned herself.

Late in the autumn, Sister Chobelet and some of the other novices were to make their vows. Just before the date chosen, one of the Fathers of the Faith then in Poitiers, Charles Gloriot, came to announce that his Society had been, after so many previous threats, finally suppressed by Napoleon, who could not rid himself of suspicions about their non-existent political influence. The group was, in fact, not to be re-formed, although most of the members found themselves again brothers in the Society of Jesus when it was revived seven years later. Father Gloriot spoke frankly to the nuns about the possibility that their Society also might be suppressed. He warned those about to make vows to consider this. They did, but were not deterred. However, the nuns' best advisers were made temporarily unavailable to them. As Superior, Father Varin tried to establish himself in Paris so as to keep in touch with his priests more easily. He was peremptorily ordered to return to his own diocese, Besançon, within twenty-four hours, under penalty of being sent to the penal colony in Guiana.

Nothing came, however, of the fear that this disaster might destroy Mother Barat's Society. In the following June, she went to Niort with Mother Geoffroy, who had just made her vows, to open the house there. Emilie Giraud, to her great grief, had been called earlier from Grenoble to take part in this foundation, and direct the school. Luckily, the children were and continued to be few, for Emilie was not yet much of a teacher. Mother Barat had written to her shortly before to remark that a cat could write better than Emilie, and that an Algonquin could spell better, and had scolded her for not working hard enough at her own education. Presumably she worked harder at Niort, and soon was intensely devoted to saintly Mother Geoffroy.

When Emilie first arrived, she found Mother Geoffroy sitting tranquilly in the woodshed, stuffing a mattress. Emilie sat down beside her, and the two began talking about God, a conversation which continued between them for years. The younger nun needed the support of affection to tide her over the first days. She was exchanging Alpine heights and horizons for a damp little house in town, where the same room was a schoolroom by day, a community room in the evening, and a bedroom at night. Food was scarce, fuel scarcer, candles few. Emilie wept for her mountain and for the great old chapel of Ste. Marie d'en Haut. But Mother Barat wrote to congratulate her on living in a house without even the necessities of life. You must be avaricious indeed, she said, in a phrase she repeated over and over again in her letters, if God is not enough for you. She wrote paraphrases of the Canticle of Canticles to her, but when Emilie became too exalted in her meditations on these, Mother Geoffroy brought her genially back to earth with the remark: "Don't spin it too fine, child, or the thread will snap and the cloth spoil. Strong thread makes good homespun."

With the end of Mother Barat's stay at Poitiers came the end of the first stage in her own history and in that of her Society. In 1808, when she returned to Amiens, she was almost thirty. Naturally and supernaturally she was now what she would always be. Her gifts had been put completely at the service of the supernatural work others had chosen for her. Since her election as Superior General, which was for life, she had had to face her responsibility in all its terrifying extent. At

Grenoble and Poitiers she had become an expert in the art of setting others on the path to holiness. Their ardor and trust had given her confidence in herself, not *as* herself, but as a tool which, she was now willing to believe, God was Himself manipulating. At Poitiers, there was a small chapel hidden in shrubbery at the end of the grounds. There she had, when she could, retired for days at a time, taking counsel for herself and for others with the only Counsellor Who would always be available. Although she would always have her moments of trembling, she was assured of a support on which she could lean.

CHAPTER SIX

1808–1816

The Constitutions

The foundation at Niort in 1808 was the sixth made by the Society of the Sacred Heart (which was still not called so openly), for Mother Baudemont at Amiens had made two before this time. One at Cuignières, near Beauvais, about thirty miles south of Amiens, had been opened as a place of refuge when there was a remote chance that the Society might be suppressed. Mother Barat had been informed rather than consulted about this, and said later that it "made no sense." Félicité Desmarquest was the Superior, and had two companions. The house was small and had been abandoned for ten years. The windows were broken and had been replaced by straw or paper. A kitchen table, a few chairs and some pots and pans were all the furnishings. Beds arrived from Amiens the day after the nuns, who had no money and no food.

However, St. Teresa on her foundations had known worse. The real trial was that, for some reason, the diocesan clergy objected to their presence and refused to allow them to go to Mass and Communion in the parish church. This complication was ironed out finally, and a little teaching and other work could be done among the neighbors.

The other foundation, at Ghent in Belgium, was made at the request of that splendid gentleman Bishop Maurice de Broglie, son of a Marshal of France. His brother Charles was one of the four who had persuaded Joseph Varin to join the Fathers of the Faith. In those early days, when an ecclesiastic to whom they had been recommended was uncooperative, Charles drew himself up and remarked that he had, as a Prince of the Empire, expected a better reception. The priest, who had not recognized him, showered him with propitiatory service, but Charles austerely refused all but the most essential, saying he would not accept as a nobleman what was refused him as a priest. To men of such temperament, one did not say no. When the Bishop asked for a foundation in Ghent, he was not refused, but the foundation was to be the cause of one of Mother Barat's most lasting sorrows. The Superior of the foundation was a twenty-one-year-old Flemish girl of Spanish origin, Antoinette de Peñaranda, a descendant of St. Francis Borgia, and the place was an old convent called Dooresele. It was Father Sambucy de St. Estève who made most of the arrangements.

Since her stay in Amiens at the time of her election as Superior General two years before, Mother Barat had been aware, partly through Father Varin and partly through the infrequency with which she was consulted about affairs at Amiens, that the estrangement between her and this first of her houses was almost complete. The younger nuns did not know her. Some of the older nuns had grown away from her in her long absence. Mother Baudemont was completely in control of her community, mostly by fear rather than love, and was herself completely under the domination of Father de St. Estève. Her assistant was his sister, a former Ursuline. Mother de Charbonnel, as head of the school, was on the Superior's Council, but she was timid by nature, and not one to interfere in the actions of those to whom she owed obedience.

It was a tour of visitation of her houses that made Mother Barat leave Poitiers for Amiens in July, taking Thérèse Maillucheau with her as companion. She would have wished to see Father Varin before she reached Amiens, but he was in Besançon and referred her to his own former teacher, Father Jean Montaigne, who had had a stormy career, and was learned and kind though unpolished. He was now director of the seminary of St. Sulpice in Paris, and the two nuns stopped off there. Father Montaigne, before letting them say a word, exclaimed: "Aren't we fortunate to have the Holy Ghost to consult!" and proceeded to tell her things about the situation in her Society which he had no natural way of knowing. He ended with the ominous but consoling comment: "There is a seed of destruction in your Society, but a soul very powerful with God is praying for you and for your Society." Mother Thérèse heard these words, and wrote them down afterward, adding the vigorous advice with which he sent Mother Barat away: "Let yourself be devoured for Jesus Christ."

She would have preferred being devoured to putting herself forward, and this preference grew when she arrived at Amiens. The first thing she noticed was that the habit had been changed, although no one had mentioned this detail to her. She said the new habit had its good points, but that she did not completely approve of it. It is well known, however, that the habit does

not make the monk. What really mattered was that neither the
school nor the community any longer followed the original
rules. Mother Deshayes tells us that, as soon as Mother Barat
went to Grenoble for the first foundation, and while Mother
Deshayes was herself still at Amiens, Mother Baudemont and
Father de St. Estève sat down to revise the rules. It was the
hodgepodge they produced that Mother Barat found in operation at Amiens. They had ignored the rules of St. Ignatius, the
basis of the original, very simple plan of the Society, and had
put together scraps from the rules of various congregations,
ending with a compilation rather than a single rule—a compilation that bore almost no resemblance to the original spirit
and form of the Society. It was in force now not only in Amiens
but in Cuignières and in Ghent.

In her instructions to the novices at Poitiers, Mother Barat
had said: "I don't know what God will do with any of you, but
I beg of you to preserve charity wherever you may be. Spread
it about at your own expense. If we can keep the bonds of
charity intact, they will support our Society, which in itself is
so small and so weak. Union will be our strength. No matter
how great the sacrifice it demands, we must keep union among
us." It was the moment to practise her own doctrine. Amiens
received her politely but formally. She was accustomed in her
houses to act like any one of the community. If you met her
sweeping the stairs, she would say: "Is it the General you want
to speak to? Just a minute till I put this broom out of sight."
Here she was treated as a visiting official, deferred to but
largely ignored. Some of her friends advised her to take a strong
stand, but that course, she saw, could have only one result—
to split the Society. It was not easy to stand still and watch the

ruin of the work she thought God wanted. But was it, she asked herself, ruin? The new way was not what she understood as the Society's way, but it was not exactly bad. What seemed chiefly compromised was her own authority. No one told her the whole truth or was quite open or honest with her. She had no specific rules to oppose to those St. Estève had made up, and she would not write any without Father Varin, whom at the moment it was not politically prudent to consult. She would let herself be devoured. She would wait. She would trust the situation to God.

Mother Deshayes was urging her to come back to Grenoble. After only a few weeks in Amiens, she went, taking Thérèse back with her. It was the beginning of three wandering years. The delight with which she was welcomed on the Mountain took away the chill of Amiens. There was Mother Duchesne teaching all day, staying up at night with sick children, managing the material details of the house, and above all yearning to go on the missions. She had Father Varin's promise that if any of them went, she would be the first chosen. She read and talked missions. She asked the children: "Who wants to go with me?" They all said they did. Some eventually would. A few years before, Mother Barat had written to her that as she stood near the harbor at Bordeaux and watched the ships, she had dreamed that the two of them were setting out to convert the savages; but for her, she knew, it was a dream only. She would prepare Mother Duchesne as well as she could to replace her. But she stayed, this time, only a month at Grenoble, and when she left it was without Thérèse Maillucheau, who was to be Mistress of Novices, and was mentioned in every letter Mother Barat wrote back. They were to take care of her, to see that she had enough sleep, that she ate well, that she was well covered up at night. She had intended to keep her with her on all her visits, but the house at Grenoble was in need, and that was more important than her comfort.

In November, she went back to Amiens alone, and had an object lesson in what St. Estève's little plots could lead to. In the old days on the Rue Neuve, Julie Billiart had come to her aid when she needed a chapel. Now, through St. Estève's efforts, Julie's congregation had been disgraced in Amiens, and she had herself been ordered out of the diocese by the Bishop, all because she stood out quietly against this egregious rule-composer's efforts to change her congregation as he had changed the Sacred Heart house in Amiens. He was against Superior Generals, for rather obvious reasons, since they could interfere with his control over houses he directed. He complained of her to the Bishop as rebellious and stubborn, and she was banished. She went quietly to Namur, but almost all her nuns followed her. This left her very necessary work in Amiens undone. The Bishop requested the Sacred Heart nuns to supply subjects to carry on the work. No one asked Mother Barat what she thought. Mother Baudemont and St. Estève chose a twenty-five-year-old novice, Marie Prévost, as Superior for the new project, and sent other novices with her to help. Letters were written back and forth, promising love and spiritual assistance between the two congregations, but Mother Barat's name never once appeared, and St. Estève was referred to as the Society's "founder."

It took the Bishop of Amiens three years to find out the truth, but when he asked Mother Julie to come back, it was too late. Marie Prévost was to return to the Society after four years, and to become one of the Society's most faithful daughters and holiest Superiors. But Mother Barat had no way of foreseeing this happy outcome as she knelt long hours in a tribune of the chapel, looking at the tabernacle and at a picture of the crucifixion: Jesus Christ present but silent, Jesus Christ suffering but not pleading His own cause. For the time being, silence was her best ally.

The next four years, while they brought much external movement, brought only imperceptible change in the situation. She was besieged by requests for new foundations, but how could she found new houses while she was uncertain whether the Society as Father de Tournély had conceived it would survive? She went back and forth over the weary coach routes from one of her houses to another, teaching and living the Society's true spirit. St. Estève, collaborating with his sister, the ex-Ursuline, and his friend Madame Baudemont, the ex-Poor Clare, and basing his work on the rule of St. Basil which is broad enough to be adapted to any spirit, slowly worked out a totally new set of rules and proposed to change the Society's name to "Apostolines." All this, including the name, was to be imposed on a Society that wanted nothing so much as to live by a rule combining the spirit of Ignatius and Teresa, and bearing the name, and breathing the gentle, loving spirit of the Sacred Heart. This was the rule and the spirit Mother Barat taught her daughters on those weary journeys.

Soon after the negotiations with the Sisters of Notre Dame, Mother Barat made her first visit to Dooresele in Ghent. She loved the fine old house, so poor that it had almost nothing in it, and wrote to Mother Duchesne that she would love this lack of comfort and convenience. She was living in a handsome room, she said, with almost no furniture. The chapel was superb, but had little else but an altar. Luckily, it needed nothing else. The nun who directed the pupils was Adrienne Michel, a sensitive and loving person, to whom we owe a series of letters from Mother Barat.

From there, she was called back to Joigny, where her father was dying. She had to leave without being with him at the end, going on to Poitiers, Niort and then Grenoble. There Mothers Deshayes and Duchesne told her how Pius VII, Napoleon's captive at Grenoble, had received the nuns and children in audience, and how, from the windows of Ste. Marie d'en Haut, they could see him every evening giving a blessing to crowds outside his prison.

The Superior General stayed on the Mountain a year. Among the pupils were many who later entered the Society and left in it names to be remembered: the two Jouve girls, who were Mother Duchesne's nieces; Julie Dussaussoy, Mother Barat's own niece; Louise de Vidaud, Josephine de Coriolis, Olympie Rombau and others.

Most of this time, Mother Barat was not well, but she still saw the children often, especially the very small ones. Her brother, Father Louis, who was always Mother Duchesne's favorite, came to give retreats and even wrote verses, of no particular merit, for convent occasions. The nuns, not too demanding, preserved them. They still survive in three carefully illuminated volumes. He strongly supported Mother Duchesne's missionary ambitions, but his sister pulled just as firmly in the opposite direction, answering Philippine's scatterbrained suggestions for immediate departure with severe if friendly comments on her lack of common sense. As she left

the house in the following November, her last reminder was
that God's work is done in the shadows and in silence.

In January 1811, she went to Cuignières, which she had
never seen. The tiny community there had not even been
allowed to communicate openly with the house at Amiens.
Since they were supposed to be holding open a place of refuge
for the Society in case of need, they must, to satisfy the St.
Estève taste for melodrama, seem to have no connection with
the house in Amiens. In this desolate condition, unable even
to make their needs known, they were, under Félicité Desmarquest, a timid but holy and practical woman, leading a poverty-
stricken and quite happy life. Mother Desmarquest often said
she had never been so happy in her life as at Cuignières. Their
spiritual director was an old priest named Lamarche, who had
been chaplain of the Carmelites of Compiègne, and had stood
at the foot of the scaffold as that martyred community went
singing to their death. He had himself escaped by one of those
inevitable stupidities of mob government which look like and
often are, from one point of view, miracles. The tiny community could help and so win the poor of the area, because a
Sister of Charity supplied them with medicines for the sick.
Mother Barat was delighted with them all. "They will be the
saints of the family if they go on like this," she wrote to Mother
Duchesne. She could not help realizing that this was, humanly
speaking, wasted suffering, but for her daughters there was
the old Ignatian parallel of watering the dry stick. Nothing
showed, but grace was there. She would have liked to stay at
Cuignières, but she knew it was not for her. She would not
have left her daughters there, either, had she had the final word

(or had she wanted just then to speak the final word) about their usefulness.

She tore herself away, looked in again at Amiens to see how things were progressing, and went back to Dooresele. There, luckily, Thérèse Maillucheau awaited her, for she fell almost at once into illness so serious that everyone feared (and she hoped for) death. It was the natural result of the moral strain of years, wearing down a frail body. However, she recovered, and wrote of her health to someone: "No doubt it is bad; but what the Lord wants will happen." Then she did the worst thing possible for her convalescence. In May 1811, she went back to Amiens.

It is true, if nearly impossible to believe, that the community at Amiens, with the exception of a very few, had no notion of the situation, which was growing always more ambiguous. How could they guess that while they lived under rules compiled by their confessor, the other houses lived by the original rule?—or that Father Varin, helped by Father Barat and sometimes by Father Julien Druilhet, was slowly evolving a more detailed version of that original rule which they had themselves almost forgotten? The younger nuns had never even known it, though they included such virtuous religious as the two de Gramont sisters, Eugénie, who had entered in 1806, and Antoinette, daughters of the Countess de Gramont d'Aster, who would shortly enter at Amiens herself.

It was on this return to Amiens that she was first allowed to see the complete rule made up by St. Estève. She found its tone disquieting, but sent it on to her brother and Father Varin. Louis Barat must have spoken his mind strongly at Grenoble on the subject, for his sister wrote hastily to Mother Duchesne, warning her and Mother Deshayes to say nothing about his disapproval. "Otherwise I should find myself in a very difficult position." But there was no use in her arguing with the authors. Her only resource was to continue, by personal contact, to try to keep up in her houses that passionate devotion to the love of Christ of which almost all trace had disappeared in the suggested rules. So she went on to Poitiers and Niort, saying nothing about the new rules, of which wild rumors were spreading, but talking constantly of the original spirit.

Back at Grenoble she fell ill again, and Mother Duchesne had the consolation of caring for her all that autumn and winter of 1811–1812. In November 1812 she wrote to Emilie Giraud, recalling their days together on the Mountain eight years before, and adding: "Since then, as you probably know, I have had little satisfaction in my life. We were children then, and Our Lord treated us as children. Now we need more solid food than milk." In the intervals when she was stronger, she finally spoke to the nuns of the new rules, showing no sign of her own opinion. But she did not have to. She had brought them up too well. They said: "We did not feel the Sacred Heart living in these constitutions, nor did we find in them the sweet, strong spirit which had chiefly attracted us to the Society."

In June 1812, for some mysterious political reason, St. Estève was jailed in Paris by Napoleon's government. Luckily, he never returned to Amiens, but he had leisure enough to polish off his masterpiece and send copies of it round to all the houses. At Amiens he was regarded as a martyr, but to their great surprise, the Dooresele community, to whom Henriette Ducis was sent to present the martyr's rules, disliked them intensely; so much so that Mother de Peñaranda, very young and not very prudent, said she would leave the Society rather than live by them. However, now everything was in the open, and Mother Barat knew that only Amiens had any desire to follow the St. Estève way. In September 1813, she named Josephine Bigeu Superior at Grenoble and set out with Geneviève Deshayes for Besançon. She and Father Varin met at his sister's country house at Chevroz, and there they completed the writing of the Society's true constitutions.

She made the trip over roads crowded with soldiers returning from Napoleon's disastrous campaign in Russia: no longer the conquering hordes which had overrun central and southern Europe, but exhausted, half-frozen, wounded. It was a moment for taking sober thought for the future. In Napoleon's empire there had been a continuation, on a more legal scale, of the anti-religious violence of the Revolution. Father Druilhet, Father Varin's collaborator on the constitutions, had spent most of the last ten years either in jail or in just escaping capture, usually for helping the Pope and the Cardinals imprisoned in France to communicate freely with each other and with the outside world. These bloody signs about her on the road to Besançon might mean that the second phase of persecution was drawing to an end, that the Church might really be free at last. Her Society must be ready to take its part in the regeneration France needed; and its part must be to spread the love of Christ.

Every moment she was not working with Father Varin she spent before the tabernacle, hour after hour, so lost in prayer that she had to be sent for to meals, and was found in the dark church, forgetful of everything but the hope that the seed of destruction might itself be destroyed.

In January 1814, she returned to Amiens. Much had changed there. St. Estève was still in prison. Marie Prévost had returned to Amiens after failing in the attempt to preserve the house of Notre Dame cut off from Julie Billiart. It had been a maturing experience, and she was quickly won by Mother Barat. Others were not so perceptive, but the community had gained at least one valiant defender of Mother Barat when the Countess de Gramont d'Aster entered.

This niece of a cardinal and former lady-in-waiting of Marie Antoinette had shared all the unreal delights of Versailles and the Trianon with her royal mistress. When that unhappy lady was in prison, the Countess wrote to her from her refuge in Germany, offering to share her humiliations also. But the Queen, now the Widow Capet, had no wish to add to the suffering which was drowning her world. The Countess, soon left a widow herself, went with her son and two daughters to England, and opened a boarding school there to support her family. Now, at forty-eight, she was learning a new way of life from her own daughter, Eugénie, who was Assistant Mistress of Novices. But she was still her daughter's superior in knowledge of people. Life at court had been an education in intrigue, and she spotted the signs even in a convent. Her chief preoccupation, however, was that the Bourbons were returning to power after the downfall of Napoleon, and might "invite" her (and royal invitations were a command) to take up her place at court. She begged, therefore, to make her vows, which would be a bar to a pious king's wishes, and she was allowed to do so in April 1814, three months after Mother Barat arrived.

For the house of Amiens, the return of the Bourbons had a

worse result. It freed St. Estève, who went off to Rome on some vague diplomatic mission, and at once, three weeks after his arrival in the Eternal City, began sending back grandiose accounts of his arrangements with cardinals and even with the Pope about the future of "his" Society. Strangely enough, all St. Estève's pet hopes for the Society seemed to be exactly what the ecclesiastical authorities in Rome wanted. A house was being opened there, which would be the mother house, under St. Estève's direct control. Everyone was delighted with the name "Apostolines." There was no possibility that any other rule than his would be approved. Mother Barat, he reported, was disregarded entirely and Father Varin considered an interloper. St. Estève summoned Mother Barat to submit to lawfully constituted authority unless she wished to ruin the whole work.

Mother Barat, not knowing what to think, wrote answers full of *politesse* but quite firm. She would be glad to sing her *Nunc dimittis,* she said, after her Society had been papally approved, but before taking final steps, would it not be wise to have the rules submitted for the whole Society's acceptance? She reminded him gently that everyone except the house of Amiens wanted a rule like that of St. Ignatius, which the St. Estève rule did not in the least resemble. Besides, since the name of Society of the Sacred Heart had been enthusiastically endorsed by everyone, might it not be hard to impose another name, no matter how attractive?

But St. Estève, meanwhile, was trying another way of furthering his cause. The Society of Jesus had been reconstituted by a papal bull in August 1814, and Father Varin had at once joined it, as had most of his brethren. Three months later, St. Estève wrote to Father de Clorivière, the French provincial, telling him about Father Varin's illegitimate interference with a Society which he, St. Estève, was trying hard to protect. But Father de Clorivière, whose long life had been constantly involved in diplomatic complications of every sort, was not so simple. He tranquilly ordered Father Varin to continue as Mother Barat's director, gave him Father Druilhet to help him with a final retouching of the constitutions, and wrote to Mother Barat: "Pray, suffer, be patient, hope," which was a summary of her conduct up to then as well as advice for the future. Father Varin, with military promptness, took up the task, writing to her: "Pax Christi! Here is the storm I have been watching gather over your head and mine for so long. Courage and confidence! Whoever asks for the cross and thinks, as you do, that you cannot live without it, must know that it is stretched out over the whole world. Let us gracefully stretch out our arms to fit it."

It was to be a cross neither one of them had expected. In Belgium, after the downfall of Napoleon, the suppressed hatred of everything French had broken out. In Catholic circles this was especially indignation at how blasphemously the French government had treated the Vicar of Christ. At Dooresele, Mother de Peñaranda, who was Flemish, and who passionately disliked St. Estève's rules, decided at this juncture that his attempt to impose them was another example of French tyranny. She had once said she would leave the Society rather than follow his rule, but she did something more ruinous: she detached her whole house from the Society.

Mother Barat wrote to warn her that the branch cut off from the vine withers. But the young Superior, though devoted to Mother Barat, yielded to the anti-French urging of the local clergy, who had good reason to distrust the French. Their bishop, the magnificent de Broglie, and two other Belgian bishops had been imprisoned in France in 1811, and forced to resign, a situation which gave rise to a schism, for most of the priests in Ghent refused to accept de Broglie's government-appointed successor.

How could Mother de Peñaranda hold out? To her later immense regret, she yielded. The French nuns in the house were recalled to Amiens. Mother Maillucheau had left earlier for reasons of health, but there still remained, among others, Adrienne Michel and Victoire Paranque, who had been assistant Superior at Dooresele. "If you have any trust in your mother," Mother Barat wrote to Mother Michel, "follow her advice. Come back with Victoire." It would be hard, of course, but "we can no longer have any joy in this world without the Cross. The Cross is the lot of those who are wedded to Christ, especially the brides of His Heart." At midnight on December 21, 1814, the first group came with Sophie Dussaussoy, Mother Barat's niece, who had been in the school. The Superior General welcomed them tenderly and saw that they were given every care after their cold and sorrowful journey.

But the shock again broke her physical resistance. Next morning another group arrived, but by then she was in bed, gravely ill. Adrienne Michel's priest brother gave her the last sacraments. Father Barat, at Bordeaux, was notified, and asked that, if she died, he be sent only a black-bordered paper. He could not bear to read the fact in words. But Father Varin, who was the more tender of the two, was also the more supernaturally straightforward. He wrote to ask her what she had ever expected of her consecration to the Sacred Heart, except a share in what Christ had received Himself? And that was suffering and betrayal by men, and apparent abandonment even by God.

Every mail brought further announcements from St. Estève in Rome. Yet she could write to Emilie Giraud: "What will come of all this? I don't know, but I find it hard to worry about it. It is possible to be saddened by what is going on, but not to be made anxious. Our kind Master will arrange nothing but for our good."

The community in Amiens were at last becoming aware of the threatened split in the Society. The nuns from Dooresele, noticing customs unfamiliar to them, asked quite innocent questions, and the Amiens religious began to suspect what had happened. Marie de la Croix, a young nun who had just made her vows, describes the atmosphere of the convent. One day, she says, when the novices were sitting quietly studying, Mother Ducis came in and said, without preamble: "Whoever is not in Peter's barque is in the sea!" and after this mysterious utterance disappeared into her own room. No one said a word, but alarms naturally rose. What and who were threatening their faith? Someone told Marie that Mother Barat, whom she loved and revered, was in danger of losing her own soul, and was leading astray those who trusted her. A recent convert to whom everything was new, Marie was appalled and perplexed.

Mother Barat, who was was not yet recovered, was not even given the care ordered by the doctor. Her presence in the house was embarrassing, and the doctor was persuaded to suggest that she be sent to Cuignières to rest. Just before she left, St. Estève had written to Eugénie de Gramont, inviting her to

come to Rome and head the new house he had established
there. Eugénie, who was much under the influence of the new
ways, hesitated. She was a strong-minded young woman, with
iron will-power that made her, in the Baudemont tradition,
rigidly virtuous. Her mother, who had not completely resigned
her parental authority, told her that if she went her mother
would go with her and open her eyes to the truth of the situation. Mother de Gramont d'Aster had also, using her high
connections, written to the French ambassador at Rome, saying courteously that the Superior General regretted her in-
ability to undertake an establishment in Rome just then.

At the beginning of August, Mother Barat at Cuignières
received from Rome a letter signed "Stephanelli, at the Roman
College," threatening her and her accomplices with excom-
munication for interfering with a work approved by the Holy
See. Unless those who sided with her submitted to the Pope
by joining St. Estève's group, they would be suppressed as a
congregation. St. Estève had guided them for ten years, and
was regarded officially, the letter said, as their founder and
superior. No one could identify Stephanelli, but everyone she
consulted took for granted that the letter was official. Father
Varin wrote that Father Montaigne thought she should return
to Amiens and tell her daughters they were free to join the
Roman house if they wished. Mother Duchesne at Grenoble
had received a copy of the Stephanelli letter, with a postscript
saying Mother Barat was no longer Superior General.

Mother Barat did not go to Amiens as Father Varin advised,
for others suggested that she wait and consult further. She herself would have submitted, had she been sure God had spoken.
But had He? Unsure, she went instead to Paris. There she

decided she would call to her the Superior and one professed nun from each house, to work for the consolidation of the Society under the rules she and Father Varin had written. She would wait and see whether any lightnings from Rome came to shatter them.

When Mother Barat left Amiens in July 1815, Mother Baudemont was no longer Superior of the community. She had made an unsuccessful attempt at a foundation in Rheims, her native place, and had then been sent to Poitiers. It was not until a year later that she left definitely for the small convent of St. Denis in Rome. In August the nuns at Amiens were told about the Stephanelli letters. Soon after, Mother Copina, the Mistress of Novices, and Mother Sambucy, St. Estève's sister, wrote formal letters to Mother Barat announcing that they were about to go to Rome.

At home, Eugénie de Gramont was confiding to Marie de la Croix that, though she loved Mother Barat, she believed her in the wrong, and was just as anxious to save her as to save herself. Marie, in desperation, turned to Mother de Gramont d'Aster, who told her frankly not to imitate her own daughters, who would live to regret what they were doing. Just then, Mother Barat invited Eugénie to Paris, with Marie as her companion, for the conference which had been decided upon.

Ten nuns came in answer to the invitation: Mother Grosier from Poitiers, with Mother de Charbonnel; Mother Bigeu from Grenoble, with Mother Duchesne, leaving Mother Maillucheau at Ste. Marie; Mother Desmarquest from Cuignières, with Mother Deshayes; Mother Geoffroy from Niort, with Emilie Giraud; and Mother Henriette Girard, the companion of that first trip to Poitiers, who came from Amiens with Mother

Eugénie. Others had disputed the advisability of asking
Eugénie, but Mother Barat hoped she could be won by kind-
ness and knew she was worth saving. The meeting began at
Mother de Gramont d'Aster's old apartment at St. Thomas of
Villanova. There was a chapel in the house containing a statue
of the Blessed Virgin before which, two hundred years earlier,
St. Francis de Sales had prayed to be delivered from despair
of his salvation, and had been answered.

Father de Clorivière, the Jesuit provincial, opened the
conference with Mass at the Jesuit house on the Rue des Postes,
and a talk on devotion to the Sacred Heart. Fathers Varin and
Druilhet spoke of the constitutions they and Mother Barat had
worked over. Everything proceeded peacefully and the constitutions were approved. On the fifteenth of December, elections were held, as the rules required, for three Assistants to the
Superior General. Mothers Bigeu, de Charbonnel and Grosier
were chosen, with Mothers Desmarquest, Geoffroy and Eugénie
de Gramont to form with them an advisory Council. Mother de
Charbonnel was made Treasurer General and Mother Duchesne
Secretary General. Next morning all renewed their vows and
signed a promise to observe the constitutions decided upon,
unless the Holy See should determine otherwise.

Two days later, Mother Barat wrote to the whole Society,
telling them what had been accomplished and assuring them
that, so far as could be ascertained, the house in Rome was
not approved and had nothing to do with the Society. The
Superiors, on their return to their houses, would give details,
she promised. The union of hearts which had been so evident
in the meeting was the work of Christ's Heart, "which breathes
only charity, and calls us to form but one heart and one soul

with His own." She ended with the words which had been placed at the end of the constitutions and were to be the motto of the Society: *Cor unum et anima una in Corde Jesu;* one heart and one soul in the Heart of Jesus.

They had decided to find a house in Paris where a Mother House and general novitiate could be established to assure a uniform religious training and so prevent any recurrence of the just-averted schism. Mother Duchesne at once went hunting and found a suitable house on the Rue des Postes. The Superiors went back to their convents with the new regulations, which were welcomed with joy. The years of indecision seemed over at last. There was only one further step to take—the winning over of Amiens. Marie de la Croix had written to Mother de Gramont d'Aster marveling at how Mother Barat made no reference to the personal insults contained in the Stephanelli letters, which now appeared so obviously the work of St. Estève under a thin Italian mask. God, said Marie, had given her back her mother. She was happy again, and she wanted to shout it abroad. She added discreetly that Mother Eugénie had also seen the light. Her sister Antoinette had been summoned to Paris after the Council. There both had heard that the Bishop of Poitiers had received an official letter from Rome saying, politely but clearly, that none of St. Estève's boasts was in the least founded. The de Gramont sisters returned to Amiens, after Eugénie had written home admitting her error. But some still doubted.

On January 23, 1816, Mother Barat arrived with Marie de la Croix. First she saw the Bishop and told him the whole story. He gave a written approbation of her rules, and said he would recognize no one as a member of her Society who did not

observe them. Mother de Gramont d'Aster has left an account
of what followed at the convent on the Rue de l'Oratoire. After
waiting some days, during which she saw in private anyone who
wished to speak to her, the Superior General summoned the
community, spoke gravely but indulgently about the diver-
gences which had existed, and promised to give a series of
talks on the constitutions. On the last day there was a general
avowal of guilt and repentance, followed by the warmest
expressions of pardon and love. On February 18, the new rules
were put in force, and no trace was left of old differences.

Or rather the trace left was good rather than bad. It
underlined the necessity of union among the religious, it
hastened the writing of the constitutions, it made clear that
the end of the Society was to be the glory of the Sacred Heart,
and it showed that such an end could be achieved only by
supernatural means. There were even naturally good results,
one of which was that the Roman authorities consulted about
the affair were amazed at the moderation with which Mother
Barat spoke of St. Estève. She had never complained or accused,
merely stated facts and asked advice. Respect for her prudence
and wisdom grew, and with it confidence in her Society.

CHAPTER SEVEN

Letters

To know how Sophie Barat had grown in the ten years of the Amiens struggle, one has only to read her letters. They say very little about external affairs, and almost nothing about the story that has just been told. They were, for the most part, letters of spiritual direction, and fall into four main cycles: the letters to Emilie Giraud, to Adrienne Michel, to Mothers Chastaignier and Balastron, and best and most numerous of all, to Philippine Duchesne.

Spiritual direction is an art rather than a science, and like any art requires a personal contribution of the artist's which cannot be taught, cannot be imitated, and can hardly even be explained. The art object aimed at is a perfect soul—not one's own, but another's. But individual souls differ in the degree of grace given them by God, and the spiritual director must work with what the soul has, as a wood carver follows the grain of the tree. To read each of these cycles of letters as a unit is to see how, teaching exactly the same doctrine, Mother Barat adapted it, with the subtlest and most graceful nuances, to each soul she handled. There are a sufficient number of scattered letters to show she was simultaneously using still other methods, as she saw them called for.

What she taught was: love Christ and imitate Him. As far

as the active work was concerned, it could be, as she explained it, summed up in the question from Proverbs: "Can a man hide fire in his bosom and his garments not burn?" If you really and practically loved Christ, the fire of love burst out in zeal. You *had* to make others love Him because you would know that was what He wanted. Conversely, if you were not trying to make others love Him, you might well question whether *you* loved Him. But if you were a religious living under rule, your zeal had to be channeled through obedience to superiors, who themselves were not free to move you in any direction except those marked out by the rules. Above all, everyone concerned must remember that the work of saving and sanctifying souls is God's work, and that therefore it is necessary to do as much as you see and trust the rest, tranquilly, to God.

With Emilie Giraud, who began as a timid, affectionate, rather clinging child, her Superior General's effort is always to give her stamina, to make her willing to give up people on whom she depends, to lead her on from a possibly sentimental attraction for feeling holy to a severely practical way of testing her devotion by remaking herself and working for others. The process is never abrupt. The letters almost always comment poetically on the Canticle of Canticles, but go on invariably, though imperceptibly, to application. Emilie has faults, which provide an excellent reason for being humble. Why has she not become so? Mother Barat tells her it is a great privilege to bring up children to love God, and adds specific directions about teaching them to speak and write and sit properly. She writes: "How little you still are! Thank God for it, since God loves the little and the simple," but "you must grow up little by little, and what a sad idea of your virtue, my dear child, your letter gives me!" When she has made her point, she ends: "Come, I don't want to scold you, or to repeat reproaches you must already have made to yourself." Elsewhere she speaks of the "little foxes" trying to devour Emilie's vines as they ripen. They are self-love, hasty snatching at what pleases her, care to avoid what is a nuisance. She urges her to watch her vineyard carefully, and knows that Emilie herself wants to do this; otherwise, what an ingrate she would be!

Often she writes in the plural: "You remember how He spoke to St. Gertrude? But we are not worthy of that; we should have to be very pure and detached from creatures to hear Jesus, and we have not yet become so." The plural, of course, deceives no one except Mother Barat herself, but the effect is encouraging. The plural makes more sense in such remarks as: "Thank God for placing contradictions in the way of all our joys, for so we are forced to look continually toward our true country and to long for it." Father Barat has been telling Emilie that it would be better to say longer prayers than occupy herself with embroidery. Mother Barat recalls how he had thrown her own embroidery in the fire as a waste of time; but, she adds firmly, "with us," embroidery is very useful, and Emilie must take advantage of every chance to learn to do it better. She must not spend too much time on it, of course. Her prayers come first, and "grammar and the other necessary sciences" next; and anyway, it is for her superior, not Father Barat, to decide whether she shall do embroidery or not.

In 1810 she comments that a letter from Emilie, though too long, was interesting, because it intermingled sense with its childishness, which did not completely hide the fact that its writer "is beginning to think in a grown-up way." Emilie has been invited to come back from Niort to Grenoble. She is happy, but regrets giving up Mother Geoffroy. Mother Barat agrees that one must always suffer in this world, and says coolly that when Emilie reaches Grenoble, "other privations await you here, and this is how we must go to Heaven." She notes that before setting out, Emilie must ask advice on how to act with the coach drivers, and in inns. But Emilie returned almost at once to Niort, and a letter tells her: "If you ever do come back to this house, you will need great virtue, and if you bring with you only the mediocre virtue you took away, it will soon be shipwrecked."

Adrienne Michel was intensely imaginative and emotional, full of exaltations and dejections, eager to read the mystical writers and to imitate their most extraordinary states. With her, Mother Barat takes a note of brisk, business-like everydayness. Adrienne is desolate because Mother Barat has left the house where Adrienne is. "The Lord is kind not to allow your Mother to stay any longer; her going was necessary; you were beginning to depend on her, and what would have become of our dear maxim: 'God alone'?" She is not to worry about her imagination. Provided her will remains steady, the obstacles raised by her imagination will only increase her merits and add lustre to her virtue. The saints had faults. The Church has canonized some of them who were very odd characters indeed. If she feels disgust and repugnance in trying to overcome herself, she must keep at it. "I have to agree with you that it is a life painful to nature," but if persevered in it leads to union with God, and that is Paradise on earth and a foretaste of heaven. But nothing extraordinary is required. Many saints have reached union with God without mystical gifts. All she is talking about is the peace of a heart that refuses the Lord nothing. If you seek only for God, you will find Him. But Adrienne must give up the taste for spiritual consolations. God is good to refuse them to her. She would become too attached to them. In the same letter she says neatly: "I was too eager to see you, and Our Lord will not let such weakness go without correction, especially since others are guilty as well as I."

Adrienne has been asking to practise severe bodily mortification. "You would like to offer the Lord a little blood from your veins," comments Mother Barat, "but is it pure enough to be offered? I don't think it is, and the self-will you put into the desire makes me sure it isn't." She must give up wanting to mortify her body and mortify her will instead. A letter begins: "I received your letter, my dear Adrienne, and I was delighted by your sufferings. See how wicked I am! My only consolation, when people become attached to me, is that they will have to make the sacrifice of their attachment." Adrienne has inquired about her health. "It is not very good," is the answer, and this is proof, offered to a Frenchwoman living unwillingly in Belgium, that France is no better for one's health than Belgium. It is silly to suppose one would be better off elsewhere. She is not to read the Apocalypse or the Canticle of Canticles, but solid works about how to practise virtue. She may learn Italian in her spare time, because it may some day be useful, but for this she is not to ask the Treasurer to buy any book for her except a grammar. As to mystical states, "if you knew how a soul can take a wrong turn in such terrible trials!" In 1814, at the height of her own worries, she writes: "We must cling to God alone, look to and hope in only God. Let the world fall apart if the Lord wishes. We must keep ourselves in peace and trust in His kindness."

Mother Balastron and especially Mother Chastaignier she treats as old friends whom she can speak to plainly. Here there is no poetic approach, no gentle teasing. She tells Mother Chastaignier: "It is a waste of time to become attached to me and to expect the least tender return from me." Either by nature or by habit—"for I can hardly think of it as a virtue"—she can think of the good her friends can do where they are, instead of the joy it would be to have them with her. Now she is delighted because Mother Chastaignier has said she will love God alone. She must not think, however, of saying long prayers. She is not up to that. She must, instead, do her duty, control her temper, hold her tongue. Mother Balastron gets the same kind of advice. Dear Balastron had promised to be more serious, but she must not work too hard at it, or be sad about it. She must be gay at community recreations, but not talk too much. Let others get a word in now and then.

Mother Chastaignier writes New Year wishes, and receives the answer that what would be appreciated most would be the wisher's conversion. She refers to some sacrifice Mother Chastaignier has tried to make without being ready for it, and compares it with offering unripe fruit. However, there is a remedy. Simply expose the green fruit to the Sun of Justice, and it will ripen fast. Why does Chastaignier not burn with the love of God? Her heart is capable of it—but her Mother must stop before saying all she would like to. Later, she writes that if Chastaignier wants to make her a gift, she should pray that God will deprive her (Mother Barat) of all consolation. But she must think twice before she asks this, because it would be a great consolation for Mother Barat to see *her,* and if God were to deprive her of this consolation!

But the best letters are those to Mother Duchesne, for here we have a saint training a saint. Mother Duchesne had her faults, but they were the positive faults of a strong character who had to be held in, kept from working herself and everyone else too hard, from being impatient with others who did not see, as she thought she did, the obvious Will of God, or if they saw it, did not move so fast toward it as she wanted to. The chief subjects of the letters in this cycle are Mother Duchesne's desire to go on the missions, her passion for long prayers and great mortifications, her affection for Thérèse Maillucheau, that woman of prayer with whom she felt thoroughly at home, perhaps the more so because she lacked Mother Barat's sound sense and moderation.

From the earliest letters, after Mother Barat's first departure from Grenoble, it is evident that the two thoroughly understand and appreciate each other. Mother Duchesne reminds her Superior that she has promised not to be put off by her faults and stop directing her. Mother Barat replies that her daughter cannot know her very well if she thinks such a promise necessary. "The Lord Who gave you to me has set no time or limits other than those of eternity. Until then if I can be useful to you, I shall be so with all my heart." Mother Duchesne must send her some linen and "pay the postage, for you know I am not rich. However, I have enough money if I use it sparingly." The package and some money have arrived, she says four days later, and after thanking her for them goes on at once to say that Mother Duchesne may stay up and pray all night on Holy

Thursday, but no one else is to do it, and she is not to try to stay awake if she feels drowsy.

Early in 1806, she answers Mother Duchesne's expression of a desire to go on the missions: "That is what I have been asking the Lord for you ever since He trusted you to me." She had once herself wanted to carry the Lord's name to the infidels, and when she came to know those Jesuits-at-heart, the Fathers of the Faith, she had made St. Francis Xavier her patron. But she has been told by "a holy soul" that she will not leave France. Now she sees that Mother Duchesne wants to go. She cannot yet say *yes,* but she tells her to hope. She must be more faithful than her Mother has been, and if she is, God may put no bounds to His mercy.

After this letter, Mother Barat never ceases to hear her cries for permission to go. It does not matter where or how. All Mother Duchesne asks is to *go.* This earns her alternate scolding and encouragement: Father Barat approves of her missionary intentions; someone has been suggesting a possible missionary opportunity; here are some missionary statistics. Meanwhile, she must learn to be a lamb, otherwise she will not make a worthy sacrifice. If she was to become a lamb first, as Mother Duchesne very well knew, she would never go, but she promised, and kept asking. Apparently she was having some minor disagreements with Mother Deshayes, her Superior at Grenoble, who was as strong-minded as she, and Mother Barat reminds her that this is not the way to become the saint she must be if she is to become an apostle. Neither should she feel sorry for herself because she has lost Mother Barat's presence. Only in heaven will they be permanently together. Since she has left Thérèse Maillucheau at Grenoble, she is sure that now at last under her, Philippine will have a good novitiate. As long as Thérèse remains, Philippine may learn from her. When she sees the trials God sends her Mistress, she is not to worry too much, for this is the price God demands of those to whom He gives great favors.

As the Society in France grew, and difficulties arose, there was less talk of the missions. Mother Barat looks forward to having Philippine as the support of her declining years, and is humiliated at how little Philippine has learned from her. When will she be docile and meek? In 1811, about the renewed desire for the missions, she writes: "How can you, at your age, be so carried away by your imagination that it blinds your judgment?" However, "that's enough. You are dear to me, and I cannot overlook your faults." She is to wish only the Will of God, and then God will do *her* will. Great projects in the future distract us from the small, necessary duties of today. In 1815, Philippine sighs for the joys of the past, and is told: "A spouse of Christ must, in this world, know nothing but the Cross. If she tries to find her joy elsewhere: *errat, errat.*"

In these letters, Sophie Barat appears as she was to be always: loving and strong; balanced and practical; not deceived by appearances, good or bad; never satisfied with the purely human; never satisfied with herself; turned always toward the Heart of Christ, and energetically insistent on turning in the same direction every heart that opened itself to her.

CHAPTER EIGHT

1816–1821

Foundations

Once the ten-years-growing threat of disunion had been finally repelled, Mother Barat had ahead of her fifteen years during which her Society could spread freely. The return of the Bourbons came just when the Society was ready to profit by the royal patronage Mother Barat recognized as useful for a work like hers, but lamented in private for its possible bad effects on her daughters. Prosperity was always a matter of alarm for her; but new works were showered with sufficient obstacles to make her feel God was with them. During these years of expansion, it was more than ever necessary to keep the Society closely connected with its center. The Paris house on the Rue des Postes, with its novitiate, was to represent this center, and there Mother Barat lived when she was not on the road visiting her houses. There she tried, when it was possible, though it usually was not, to keep one of her assistants. There also she kept from the beginning Eugénie de Gramont, whose firm hand and aristocratic connections were to insure the temporal success of the Paris boarding school for almost thirty years.

Before Mother Barat settled down in the Rue des Postes, with Mother Duchesne as the Secretary of the Society, she had overseen the moving to Beauvais of the house at Cuignières, and visited Amiens, Poitiers and Niort, where the nuns had finally left their damp little house for the large one they had wanted eight years earlier. She reached Paris at the end of June, 1816, and found that Mother Duchesne, alone with two young religious, had been in her element, painting, whitewashing, helping the masons and glaziers, with the skill she had learned in repairing Ste. Marie. Some novices were sent from Amiens and Grenoble, and there were two postulants. The presence of Eugénie de Gramont attracted the best families, although they could not awe a de Gramont, and awed still less the barrel maker's daughter from Joigny who, then and always, saw the little rich girls in her schools as children to be pitied for the temptations to which their position left them open.

During those early months in Paris, Mother de Gramont learned to know and love the Superior General she had been so willing to shake off not so long before, and was periodically overcome by remorse for the past. This remorse was kept active by a renewed appearance of the former confessor of Amiens. Mother Sambucy had died in Rome, and her brother now began litigation about her effects. Eugénie had to go to Amiens to see about this, and wrote letters of complete repudiation to the priest who had so influenced her. The experience so shook her that her never robust health was affected. Mother Barat wrote to her over and over again that she was to forget the past. God, she reminded her, judges our intentions, and Eugénie's intentions, she was sure, had always been good. She had been young, and had allowed herself to be led astray. Would she ever have learned how much Mother Barat loved her, if they had not gone through this sorrow?

Eugénie's mother was to be Superior of a foundation in Brittany, at Quimper, on the farthest northwestern tip of France. But Josephine Bigeu was sent to begin the foundation, as she did so expertly and often in the too short time she was to be spared to Mother Barat.

But more important than any other event in the lull after the coming to Paris was the sacrifice for which Mother Barat had been training Philippine Duchesne, and which at last took place less than two years after Philippine had made ready the Mother House. In January 1817, Bishop Dubourg of Louisiana came to the new convent of the Sacred Heart asking for missionaries for his diocese. Mother Duchesne was portress. As soon as she heard the visiting prelate's name, she decided she had an obvious sign of the Will of God. Mother Barat, however, said she would not bring the question up unless he did, and that in any case it would need eighteen months to work something out. When the Bishop got round to the reason for his call the next morning, she told him about Mother Duchesne. He was delighted, and asked to see her. She was not hard to find. The Bishop went off to Belgium and came back in May, but Mother Barat had not yet made up her mind. Philippine pursued them to the door when he was leaving, threw herself on her knees, and begged to be sent. All her passionate desire, so long and so badly repressed, burst out unchecked. Mother Barat could not resist. She promised to send to Louisiana the following spring a band of missionaries which would include Mother Duchesne. Meanwhile there was the foundation at

Quimper, and illness in the community made it possible that
the ranks would be thinned.

May 1818 was the tentative date set for Philippine's great
adventure, but in January, Bishop Dubourg's vicar general,
Father Martial, announced he was leaving from Bordeaux in
February and would expect to find the missionaries ready.
Mother Barat put Mother Duchesne in charge of the material
arrangements for the departure. Four religious were to ac-
company her: Mothers Eugénie Audé and Octavie Berthold,
and two coadjutrix sisters, Catherine Lamarre and Marguerite
Manteau. By the seventh of February, the little group were in
Paris. Octavie, who was thirty, had been converted from Cal-
vinism at the age of twenty, had entered at Grenoble three years
before her departure for the missions, had been sent to Paris
when the house was opened there, and had made her vows only
a year ago. She was a beautiful woman, with a lovable dis-
position, and a precious aptitude for foreign languages, which
Mother Duchesne did not share. Octavie had no particular attraction for the missions, but made the sacrifice of France in
gratitude for her conversion. Mother Audé, who had been at
the foundation of Quimper, was another Grenoble novice transferred to the Rue des Postes. A rather flighty but affectionate
and generous girl, she had brought worldly tastes to the novitiate from her socially successful debut in Italy and France, and
she made over her habit to show off her figure. The austere
Father Roger's 1816 retreat had even more completely made
her over, and it was a humble, mortified religious who prepared to set out for Louisiana. She had had to be sent for at
the last moment from Quimper. There was some doubt that she
would arrive in time, but she did, and made her last vows on

the morning she left. The two Sisters were older, and their contribution, under the primitive conditions in Missouri, was to
be invaluable.

Mother Barat told them that if they accomplished nothing
except to set up one tabernacle more in which Christ could live
among men, they would have done enough. She gave them
everything she could think of to make their life more livable
in the mysterious, far country. Philippine would have been
completely happy except for one circumstance: she had been
named Superior. Mother Barat had told her over and over how
much she needed to be guided, how disastrous it was for her
to rely on herself. Now, when she was going so far away from
everyone on whom she did depend, when months must elapse
before advice could come to her from France, she must, under
unexampled conditions, depend upon herself—or better, on
God alone. It was for this moment Mother Barat had been
training her, trying to root out all self-assurance and fondness
for her own way. She would never again, she thought, be
tempted to such faults; but left with only God and herself, she
saw, for the first time since the dark days before Mother Barat's
coming, how bleak and dangerous it was to make lonely decisions. She was given exceptional powers, made necessary by
the distance from France, and this terrified her even more.
Mother Barat knew exactly what she was suffering, but knew
it was necessary. She had realized since her brother routed her
out of her games at Joigny that there is no unmixed joy in this
life.

Mother Barat wrote to her at Bordeaux: "Work hard to be
every day more deserving of this work, by building up, on the
foundation of humility, the gentleness and forbearance you

must practise toward those trusted to you." Philippine must tell
her on what day the ship was to sail, so that the two friends
could say in their hearts a farewell which might be their last
in this world. In Bordeaux, the missionaries stayed in the same
convent where Father Roger had gathered Thérèse Maillucheau and her friends twelve years before to meet Mother Barat.
Mother Duchesne's greatest supporter and favorite director,
Father Louis Barat, was in Bordeaux, and that was a great comfort. They paid their respects to Archbishop d'Aviau, who had
been so reluctant to let his pious little flock go off to Poitiers.
It was not, actually, until the twenty-first of March, six weeks
after they left Paris, that the *Rebecca* sailed. There was only
one priest on board, and the trip lasted three weary months.

Mother Barat was in her thirty-ninth year when Philippine
Duchesne left for America. When she turned back to the house
on the Rue des Postes, after the missionaries' carriage was out
of sight, she was, in a way, beginning a new life of her own.
She had reached the full development of spiritual maturity, of
which the test is the power to face anything without being
shaken by it. In her case, it was a combination of natural and
supernatural gifts which gave her this power, a combination of
natural and supernatural balance. She could suffer and was still
to suffer intensely, but she could do so serenely. The departure
of Philippine Duchesne deprived her of one of the few to whom
she spoke freely of her spiritual life; but she could at least, she
said, create a solitude in her heart, and if God did not yet reign
there as Master, at least the place was free, and she could go on
making it more and more accessible to Him. She had written
to Thérèse Maillucheau two years before that she went about
saying to everything she saw: "No, you are not my God."

She had often to say it, these days—and said it with little difficulty—of the great personages who frequented the Rue des
Postes, and insisted upon seeing the Superior General: present
or future bishops, members of noble families, and others to
whom courtesy was due. If it had not been so clearly due,
Mother Barat would have escaped it, for this kind of thing
only took from the time she saved for God and her daughters
and her children. Eugénie de Gramont did the honors whenever it was possible for her Superior to escape. Eugénie, though
she was very small and somewhat deformed, did not need to
rely on her name to win respect. She was a powerful, tactful
person, with capacity for managing others, and the courage
and devotedness of a religious added to the manners of a great
lady. Mother Barat, who knew her best, lavished affection on
her, but was not unaware of her faults: her incomplete religious
education in the Baudemont-St. Estève school, her temptation
to dominate as well as a tendency to be too much led, her con-
sciousness of her birth and talents. Mother Barat's letters to
her, during the thirty years Eugénie was Mistress General, then
Superior and finally Superior Vicar in Paris, show her persistent
effort to win and to guide this dangerously gifted woman, to
prevent her making other mistakes more disastrous than that
she was bewailing in the early days at the Rue des Postes.

That mistake sent up still another echo presently. A founda-
tion was being made in Chambéry, in Savoy, southeast of Lyons.
On the way there, Mother Barat stopped in Grenoble, and saw
Mother Duchesne's niece, the candid, charming Euphrosine
Jouve, now a young religious who had changed her name to
Aloysia. To Mother Barat's grief, she had contracted a mysteri-
ous but apparently incurable disease. Aside from her sorrow at

the girl's suffering, Mother Barat was not unaware that she "was the only one with superior talents, one who would have been so useful for foundations."

On July 21, she went on to Chambéry with Mothers Bigeu and Maillucheau. They had hardly arrived when Mother Baudemont, who had succeeded Mother Sambucy as Superior of the convent in Rome, appeared in Savoy, trying to find subjects for her languishing house. She spoke to the Bishop and all the prominent people who had before been anxious to have the Society, convincing them that Mother Barat's nuns were a severed branch of her own society, and the weary process of unmasking her had to be gone through again. Morever Mother Baudemont was claiming the return of money, books and relics she had contributed to the Society. She came in person to call on Mother Barat, who said she would not have charity wounded for the sake of money, and agreed to all she asked. But finally everything was cleared up, and Mother Barat's only comment was: "We must not speak ill of these people."

There were other complications, of the sort familiar in new houses. The priest who had first persuaded them to come tried to have too much control over them, and resented their objecting. They had finally to buy a new house. The financial burdens were immense and there was even a lawsuit. But this was the atmosphere to be expected in foundations—the difficulties which guaranteed good to come. On her way to Chambéry, she stopped at Grenoble, and from there wrote to Emilie Giraud: "Do you remember my first arrival on the mountain? You were there then, and it was not always a mountain of myrrh; it was sometimes a little Thabor. All that is over. I could stay only twenty-four hours, and then hastened to Savoy to fill my hands with thorns."

The same year, she made a foundation near Lyons, at La Ferrandière, with Mother de Charbonnel, this time, handling the details. She wrote to Mother Duchesne afterward: "We must stop now, for a few years, and try in the meantime to become holy, and prepare ourselves to carry out the plans of God." But Archbishop d'Aviau, who could hardly be put off a second time, after so many years, wrote to her about a Madame Lalanne, a widow, who had founded a small congregation to bring up orphans, and who wanted to fuse her congregation with the Society. The Archbishop made the suggestion diffidently, feeling this little group were perhaps not grand enough. Mother Barat set him right, writing to him that although she had intended not to make another foundation for two years, the simplicity, humility and poverty of Madame Lalanne's sisters attracted her as brilliant offers could not. Mother Geoffroy was sent from Niort to arrange matters. Madame Lalanne, though she was sixty-two, was received into the Society and left as Superior of the house. Mother Barat put her under obedience to take whatever measures her age and ill health demanded, told her she might go on giving presents to her nephew, and refused to allow her to change her will in favor of the Society, since her relatives needed the little she could leave them.

It was not that the Society could not have used the money, however little. In Paris, the house on the Rue des Postes had proved too small, and they had been forced to buy for the novitiate the house next door, which had once belonged to the Jacobin Santerre. Mother Deshayes was put in charge of the novices. She, who had sold all her pretty dresses to keep the first house in Amiens out of debt, was now teaching these young women, who had presumably sold all they had, how to buy the pearl of great price.

At Grenoble, all during this year, Mother Thérèse Maillucheau was making the Society's financial position even more insecure by her instinctive inefficiency.

There was also disquieting news from America. Mother Barat had understood that her nuns were to have a house in the capital of Missouri, St. Louis. Instead they were relegated to a village, St. Charles, where they would be of no use. There was no money, there were no boarders, there was no credit. Mother Barat wrote to their bishop, and they were transferred to Saint Ferdinand, which was presumably better, but which turned out to be just as bad. They moved on Christmas Eve, 1819, and had midnight Mass when they arrived.

The greatest sorrow of that year and the year following was the illness of Aloysia Jouve. After her childhood at Ste. Marie, Euphrosine had returned to her family in Lyons and refused the usual "good matches" before entering at Grenoble. Mother Barat spoke of her as the hope of the Society; Mother Duchesne confidently expected her to join her on the missions, but Aloysia herself had always felt she would die young. Three months after her vows she suffered from pains in her foot. The foot soon broke out in open sores which spread to the rest of her body. The doctors were baffled. From Paris, where she was at the time, Mother Duchesne wrote letters both tender and bracing.

Mother Barat, not yet resigned, tried every expedient. When she came to Grenoble in June 1818, after not having seen Aloysia in three years, she was shocked to see the young nun dragging herself about on crutches. She allowed her to make her final profession several years ahead of the regular time, but there was no effect on her increasingly wounded body. The last months she spent in bed in a state of complete helplessness and complete happiness. On the feast of St. Agnes, January 21, 1821, she died, as she had predicted, at twenty-five, the same age as St. Aloysius Gonzaga.

No one doubted that she had gone straight to heaven, and from there she won vocations to the Society for her two sisters, one of whom, Amélie, followed her aunt to America. Her brother, who had given up the practice of his faith, was converted on seeing her body, and became a Jesuit. Miracles were so numerous that crowds flocked to the convent wanting to see the young nun's resting place in the vaults under the old monastery. Father Roger, that stern lover of the hard and the humble, said to Mother Barat: "What's this I hear? Has your Aloysia taken to miracle making? Soon your nuns will be eaten up with pride!" Mother Barat, completely agreeing, begged Aloysia to discontinue her favors. The miracles stopped. This detail of the story is not *de fide*; but certainly Mother Duchesne would have disapproved if, under the circumstances, the miracles had *not* stopped.

In America, Mother Duchesne was sure Aloysia was responsible for the first influx of vocations there, and for the successes which came, within a few years, to Mother Audé in Louisiana. Almost no success came to Aunt Philippine in Missouri, but it is hard even for a miracle-worker to arrange success for an aunt so obsessed with the desire for humility that she prays for contempt. However, Mother Audé had the success, which took care of the spread of the work, and Mother Duchesne received the contempt, which made a saint of her.

Grief for the death of young nuns runs like a refrain through all Mother Barat's story. Novices take so long to train, and they die as soon as they are in active life, or sometimes before reaching it. It is all very well for them. They are in heaven, and she does not begrudge them their bliss. But if God wants foundations, as the number of requests seems to indicate, why does He not leave her her nuns?

CHAPTER NINE

1821–1828
The Hotel Biron
and the Trinità

The third decade of Mother Barat's Society began in 1820 with the acquisition of one of its most impressive schools. The buildings on the Rue des Postes were not big enough and Mother Barat, with the approval of her Council, began looking for a large, plain house. Paris was not the best place to combine these requirements. Big houses were not plain, nor plain houses big. The house they bought was big, but far from plain. It was the Hotel Biron on the Rue de Varenne, built in the eighteenth century by the same architect who designed the Petit Trianon and the north side of the Place de la Concorde. The property was offered to them at a reduced rate, but even that was far outside their range. Mother Barat's Council decided to ask help from the King. To make the request, they chose a novice who had just given up being a court lady. She was the Comtesse de Marbeuf, who was then fifty-five, widow of a man Louis XVI had made governor of Corsica. There she had known the Bonapartes, and so was able to return from exile when Napoleon came to power. Louis XVIII gave a hundred thousand francs, the rest was borrowed, despite Mother Barat's thrifty horror of debts, and the house was bought.

The community and school moved in as soon as drastic alterations had been carried out. Mirrors, pictures, gilded ornaments were ruthlessly sacrificed. The children were lodged in the regular living quarters of the house, and the rest of the handsome part became classrooms and study halls and parlor. The nuns retired to the servants' quarters and the stables. Mother Barat was not happy about increasing grandeur. Once, before the removal to the new house, a Duke came to call on her about raising funds for the purchase. He found her at the front door, replacing one of the Sisters at cleaning up. The gentleman observed for a while the unexpected sight of a Superior General vigorously using her broom. Then he said genially: "Ah, Madame Barat, I have caught you in the act. What are you doing?" She answered coolly: "What I should have spent my life at, if I had been left where I belong." Then with as much self-possession as the Duke's own, she ushered him into the parlor she had just swept, to discuss how to raise seven hundred thousand francs to buy a medium-sized palace.

It was some consolation, when the moving was complete, to look at the doors of the small, low-ceilinged rooms occupied by the nuns and see the signs: "Groom, Barber, Cook," indicating the rank of previous occupants. She wrote to Mother Audé in the American wilderness: "Thank God we are no better off in the Hotel Biron than anywhere else." And there were, of course, debts to be paid. Responsible chiefly for paying them was Mother de Charbonnel who, while engaged in these large financial transactions, lavished time on such important jobs as helping the novices spread out the washing to dry. In the winter, a novice tells us, "the washing used to freeze, and our hands, too." Then the Treasurer General would say to the "more delicate and less courageous," "Go and get warm," while she stayed until the job was done.

In April 1822, Mother Barat wrote to Philippine Duchesne that there were already "ninety families to be seen, heard, written to," and added: "How we should prefer to evangelize the savages!" They would not be so inclined, she explained, to throw away the grace offered them as were the daughters of "nobles, ministers, etc." However, in honesty she admitted: "We have some children who are good and solid; but what trouble and care it all takes!" The worst trouble was spending hours in the parlor with noble relatives.

Nor were the callers confined to the families of the children. Occasionally Madame Félicité de Genlis, in the last decade of her long life, called at the Rue de Varenne to share her views on education. She had, after all, brought up Louis-Philippe, who was to come to the throne the day after she died, and few were more expert on the bitter intrigues of court life into which many of the demoiselles at the Hotel Biron were to move. Madame de Genlis, as a novelist of the more obvious school, must have appreciated the contrast between Mother Barat and herself. Madame de Genlis had devoted herself to getting on in the right circles, and tried with uneven success to teach her pupils how to do the same. Mother Barat did her best to keep the values and ambitions of the "right circles" out of her pupils' minds. She would not have exaggerated elegance in dress (although the young ladies were not to look dowdy, either) and she forbade the complicated hair arrangements which took too much time and drew too much attention.

Pride was the young ladies' besetting sin: pride of birth, rank, fortune, pride in their more exalted friends, even pride in the social standing of the nuns who taught them. Once, before the move to the Hotel Biron, they complained that one of the teaching nuns was not of noble birth. Mother Barat went to them, spoke with deceptive mildness of the respect due to religious, and added that apparently they did not share this respect. So they wanted only noble ladies to teach them? Very well, then they could do without her, since she was far from noble. "Goodbye, young ladies, this is the last you will see of me." This threat brought them round.

When some young lady was guilty of worse sins than this kind of pride, Mother Barat was ruthless. She did not tolerate unworldly innocence in those dealing with the children. They must be able to recognize vicious influence when they saw it, and pupils who exercised it were to be sent away at once. On the other hand, mere high spirits and rebellion against regulations were more indulgently handled. Mother Barat often took over a small group of the more fiery youngsters and gradually tamed them, lessening the strain at first and then leading her noisy remnant to control themselves through supernatural motives. There was never any doubt that this self-control was necessary. Madame de Genlis had herself taught her charges to be self-controlled and endure hardships if necessary. The day and night difference between the two systems lay in the end each had in view.

But nothing could be less rigid than Mother Barat's directions about caring for the children. Her letters are full of minute suggestions on the subject. Mother de Gramont, she writes to her, is kindness itself when the children are really ill but is apt to brush off minor indispositions. This is not right. She owes it to the children's families to see that they are protected. In the hot weather, she writes that they are to be given apricot juice, or water with a *very* little wine. The nuns are, in short, to be mothers to the children, and even to the older girls, and one way to turn Mother Barat from a lamb to a lion was to neglect her precious flock.

Between 1815 and 1830, when the next revolution in France again threatened to destroy the Society, twenty foundations were made, six of them in the United States. In 1821 Mother Bigeu, already suffering from the illness which would prevent her surviving this decade, had gone to Le Mans with Eugénie de Gramont to examine a Benedictine monastery that had been offered them. It was accepted, and Eugénie's mother left Quimper to become its Superior. A few months later, Mother Barat was writing to Mother Duchesne about a house at Autun which, she said, being half-way between Lyons and Paris, would be very useful. There Mother de Charbonnel took over a former Visitation convent, cleaned up the mess left by soldiers who used it during the Napoleonic wars, and gave over its direction to Victoire Paranque, one of the French nuns rescued from Dooresele. Father Varin brought his niece, Aglaë Varin, to be one of the first pupils, till a school could be opened in Besançon, the Varins' home city. She later became a member of the Society and one of those young nuns who went to heaven too rapidly.

It was from Dooresele itself that Mother Barat received reinforcements as well as great joy during 1823. Two years before, the rulers of Belgium had passed restrictive laws which seriously impeded the work of religious education. At the time, the Mistress General of the Dooresele school was young Louise de Limminghe, who had made her vows the day before the community broke its connection with Mother Barat. She had not been told about this until after her vows, and when she understood it, could not reconcile herself to the new state of affairs. However, she felt herself bound, and it was not until Mother de Peñaranda told her community that they were free to withdraw if they were unwilling to accept the new government restrictions, that she decided to return to the Society. The Belgian clergy forbade any such move, and she was refused the sacraments by the confessor, but she persisted, arrived in Paris in October 1822, and was received by Mother Barat with some reserve, at first, but with great kindness. The reserve soon vanished, and Mother de Limminghe, despite her experience and former office, was sent to relearn religious life under Mother Desmarquest, the newly appointed Mistress of Novices.

Affection soon inspired her to urge Mother de Peñaranda to follow her example. The house at Dooresele was by now disbanded, and though the Superior and her assistant, Henriette Coppens, had tried to found elsewhere, they had not succeeded. Mother de Limminghe's letter persuaded them to return, though they still thought the French untrustworthy. They came, however, and seventeen of the Dooresele community followed them. Henriette Coppens became a much-loved Mistress of Novices and Treasurer General, and Mother de Peñaranda was soon appointed Superior. The generosity of Mother Barat in trusting such offices to women who—as others might

have put it—had once failed her, was of a piece with her ordinary way with people.

She usually paid a high price for her consolations. In 1821
Father Montaigne, whom she called "the only one who thoroughly understood my soul," died in Paris. She wrote to Emilie
Giraud: "I shall miss his direction, but God alone, now! He
wants our whole heart for Himself." In December she quoted
St. Augustine to Mother Chastaignier in the same vein: "He
loves Thee less, my God, who with Thee but not for Thee loves
something else." In June 1822, her mother died at Joigny, with
her Jesuit son beside her. Mother Barat wrote to Thérèse Maillucheau to ask prayers—"the only consolation I can have in
such great suffering." In September, after stopping off at the
empty house in Joigny on her way from Autun, she wrote to her
nephew, Father Louis Dussaussoy: "How everything changes,
and passes away! May you come to see the earth as I see it,
only as a place of exile."

She came near leaving this place of exile when, in the following March, she fell ill at Grenoble, where she had gone on a
mission that could hardly attract her. In her long period of
government, Mother Thérèse had been far from a success. By
her impractical generosity toward every need she saw or suspected, she had brought the house near financial ruin. And
there were other administrative troubles. Mother Barat loved
and admired Thérèse intensely, and knew she was holy. How
to give scope to her spiritual influence without exposing a
house to material disaster remained one of her problems until,
after some years, she decided that Thérèse's kind of light could
shine more successfully from under a bushel than from a candle-
stick. She had not yet reached that conclusion, and was about

to change her from Grenoble to Quimper, where she would have nothing to do with finances or the school. She had, no doubt, some necessary but unattractive truths to expound before sending her to this restricted apostolate in Brittany, and she did not look forward to the business.

It was March, but the mountain and even the valley were under snow. Winter was always a dangerous season for Mother Barat. She wrote to her nephew that she wanted "to forget all that belongs to earth and to think of heaven, where everything suggests we shall soon return." A few days later, she was so seriously ill that the doctors held out no hope. Mothers de Charbonnel and de Gramont came to her but another Physician had His own plans. Her fourteen-year-old niece, Dosithée, youngest of her sister's daughters, all of whom she had admitted gratis to her schools, was at Beauvais. She was far from being a morbid child, and had much of her aunt's intelligence and gaiety. Her priest uncle was very fond of her and looked forward to making her a replica of her aunt. Having no doubt read of such things in pious books, she offered her life for her aunt's. Shortly thereafter she died, and her aunt promptly recovered. It is a story which some will find disturbing, and about which others will say: *Post hoc ergo propter hoc?* But the fact remains. Her aunt would have been the last to think the sacrifice worth it, but would certainly not doubt the possibility.

She had hardly recovered when she undertook a foundation at Besançon which was to give the Society its second Superior General, Josephine Goetz, an Alsatian, who was about six years old when the house was opened in 1823. Another house, in Turin, the capital of Piedmont, was requested by the King and Queen, operated under the close though benevolent watchfulness of those pious monarchs, and lodged superbly. Mother Bigeu, in one of her intervals of health, made the arrangements, and Mother de Limminghe was sent there to become, eventually, Superior. Registration was restricted to noble families and important legal and military families. This aristocratic tie-up was to be the downfall of the house, which was swept away in the 1848 revolutions.

In 1825, Josephine Bigeu was sent to Rome, where there was not yet a Sacred Heart convent, to negotiate Papal approbation for the Society. She stayed a year, with only two companions, trying to hurry the authorities, who had not the least intention of hurrying, suffering much from illness, but reviving sufficiently to accomplish her assignment. By the autumn of 1827 she was so ill that only a miracle could save her, and Mother Barat tried her best to obtain the miracle. Her letters were full of this anxiety. "How touched you would be by her patience!" she wrote in October to Mother Duchesne who had just, in dire poverty, opened the much wanted house in St. Louis; but she knew Philippine would share her concern for this irreplaceable old friend. "I have to admit," she said, "that the life of a Religious of the Sacred Heart, and especially of a Superior, is a long martyrdom, particularly as you near old age and live long enough to see those you love and have lived with die." To Henriette Grosier, who had just been sent to Bordeaux, she wrote at the same time: "She is suffering dreadfully, but nothing is too much for her patience." She orders the two houses in Bordeaux to join in a novena for the cure, and adds: "What intense grief I feel at seeing her suffer so without being able to relieve her! Pray for your Mother. You must realize what this costs her."

At the end of November, another letter to Mother Duchesne tells the failure of all her efforts to save Mother Bigeu. "I do not mention my sorrow," she wrote, "for you no doubt understand it." She had recently lost another Superior, Cécile Camille, at whose deathbed Mother Bigeu had spent her last energies. The double loss was crushing, and she wrote to Emilie Giraud that God was punishing them for their lack of cooperation with His graces. There were so few generous and faithful souls. One would be enough to appease His anger. She saw herself as most in need of punishment, not fit to turn away wrath. At the end, when Mother Desmarquest brought her novices to see her, Josephine Bigeu, remembering her years of labor and illness, had said: "If they knew how happy I am at this moment to have left all for God!" She was only forty-nine years old. After her twenty years in the Society, full of hard and successful work, Mother Barat's last word about her was: "What wounds me most is that we have lost a soul perfectly adapted to the work of God . . . just when the needs of the Society are most pressing."

Less than a year later, she was to lose another old friend, Henriette Girard, who had chaperoned the trip to Poitiers.

This currency of suffering, always more plentiful in the Society than the usual kind, enabled her to purchase two of the Society's best foundations in the years just before and just after Mother Bigeu's death. The first was in Lyons. Mother Geoffroy was called from Niort, leaving her dear daughter Emilie Giraud there as Superior, and became the spiritual guide of half the noble ladies of Lyons as well as of the new house. This was in April, 1827.

Of the other foundation, Mother Barat wrote in January,

1828 to Armande de Causans, another court lady who had, at the age of thirty-six, entered the Paris novitiate in 1822. She was now Superior of the house in Turin, tactfully handling their royal patrons, who had a way of dropping in and wanting to sit in on classes to see how their little countesses were being prepared for the great world. The French government, Mother Barat told her, owned in Rome a beautiful house with enormous gardens on the Pincian hill. Pope Leo XII had asked the King— by now Charles X—to give this property with part of the revenues to the Religious of the Sacred Heart, so that they might do for the young ladies of Italy what they were doing for those of France. It was Archbishop—later Cardinal—Luigi Lambruschini, Apostolic Nuncio at Charles X's court, who had made the suggestion, after he had observed the "order, excellent manners and piety" of the pupils at Turin, and had made the acquaintance of Mother Barat in Paris.

The house in question was the fifteenth century monastery and church of the Trinità dei Monti at the top of the Spanish steps, near the lodgings where the poet Keats had only a few years before ended his brief career. In a few months, Mother de Causans was expediting affairs in Rome. The great difficulty, she wrote, was that everyone, thinking the Sacred Heart nuns were wealthy, charged them extra, and no one dreamed of helping them.

In November a specially picked group of twelve foundresses led by Mother de Charbonnel set out for Rome. One was a Russian princess, Elizabeth Galitzin, who had not yet made her vows. She had been converted by Father Rozaven. Mother Barat wrote to Rome: "The Sacred Heart has given us a great grace by placing us so near the Head of the Church," and said they must show their gratitude by being humble lovers of poverty and contempt. She added: "Just now, in France, we are showered with contempt. It is frightful. Evil men are responsible for it. We bear it and it is a grace we must try to take advantage of."

CHAPTER TEN

1828–1832

Revolution

This contempt was not for the Society itself but for religion in general. It was too much to expect that government support of religion, even backed as it had been by the missionary work of the Jesuits and other congregations, could root out the anti-religious feeling which had brought havoc on France at the end of the eighteenth century. In 1828, the year of the foundation in Rome, religious teaching was restricted, and the Jesuits were forced by royal order to close their schools. This concession on the part of a friendly government was a symptom of its weakness and a presage of its fall.

Mother Barat, to whom rumor and fact poured in through the parlors of the Rue de Varenne and through Father Varin, Superior of the Jesuit house in Paris, knew catastrophe was imminent, and dreaded it, for her houses were increasingly prosperous, just then, and vocations many. She wrote to Mother Duchesne in June 1828: "We are on the verge of great calamities." Father Varin told the Paris community that persecution was certainly near, but reminded them that the servants were not greater than their Master, and pointed out that persecution for His name was glorious. He added gaily that, in the twenty-eight years since he and his priests had returned from Germany, his Society had been dissolved four times. Why not a fifth?

Mother Barat urged her daughters "in these frightful times," with their scandals and abominations, to offer themselves as victims for the sins of the world, and wrote to Emilie Giraud, now bearing the burden of the house in Niort, that extraordinary times called for extraordinary virtue. Nevertheless, foundations went on: one in Perpignan, where the city authorities gave the property, and one in Avignon, the old city of the Popes.

In May 1829, Mother Barat had what seemed a minor accident, a fall which injured the nerves of her foot. Actually, the injury was to make walking impossible for her during more than three years—years when she had to travel farther and more frequently than at any time in her life. The doctor told her that unless she wanted the foot to "become a specimen in my collection," she had best stay completely still. Nine months later, in February 1830, she wrote to Mother Duchesne that she was still in bed, or carried about in a basket, or dragging herself on crutches, and that the doctors said she must look forward to at least three months more of this. She confessed she was afraid it might last the rest of her life. Her helplessness left her at the mercy of others for every move, and this must have been a torment for anyone so swift in thought and act; but she bore it lightly, not complaining when she was left waiting because someone had forgotten her. The Sister who cared for her was a good and willing soul, but neither a skilful nurse nor an attractive character. Her patient refused to have her changed.

In May 1830, Mother de Gramont received the Duchess of Berry, who brought the Queen of Naples to visit the Rue de

Varenne, and was "full of hope for the religious future of France," which Mother Barat, whose injured foot gave her an excuse for avoiding the royal visitors, was not naïve enough to share. On the feast of St. Mary Magdalen, July 22, there was much decorous rejoicing for the Superior's name day. But the Superior looked through tears at the one hundred and sixty pupils, and told Mother de Gramont it was the last time she would see them all together. The remark needed no gift of prophecy. Next day Father Varin came for the school holiday and asked the novices whether they were ready for martyrdom. Being novices, they were exalted by the thought, and ran to tell Mother Barat, still in her room, about the prospect. She was glad they were willing to endure it, but remarked that it was still necessary to take precautions to escape it.

On July 27, riots began. Some parents took their children away. Next day the nuns heard the sound of cannon. Mother de Gramont, who was not well, had gone from Paris to the nearby village of Conflans, where Hyacinthe-Louis de Quélen, Archbishop of Paris, offered her the use of a small house belonging to the archdiocese. Mother Barat's counsellors decided to send her to Conflans, for her infirm condition would be an embarrassment in case of trouble at the Hotel Biron. With one Sister and her nephew Stanislaus as escort, she arrived without incident at the little house on the slope above the Seine, from which she could look across at the city. It was thirty-six years since she had first seen Paris as a little country girl coming up to the capital. For twelve years now, in spite of constant journeys, it had been her only fixed home since Joigny.

The first night was far from restful. The four nuns were alone in the isolated house, the fourth being a very young nun, Anna de Constantin, niece of the Count de Maistre who had had such high hopes of the good effects of revolution in France, "the finest kingdom after the kingdom of heaven." Mother Barat and Mother de Gramont stayed up all night praying that the noise might not mean what they thought it meant. Next morning, the twenty-ninth, they learned that the nearby seminary had been abandoned, and that they were quite alone. Early in the afternoon a mob almost attacked the house, thinking priests were in it, but they fortunately changed their collective mind. Another night in the exposed house was not to be thought of. Mother de Constantin and Sister Rosalie, in secular dress of a not too fashionable sort, went out to look for safer lodging. Even at this juncture, Mother Barat could burst out laughing at the sight of her oddly-dressed daughters. A charitable lady finally took them all in for the night, but for a night without sleep, full of the noise of fighting in the city.

On the thirty-first, the Paris gardener came to announce the government had fallen. France had no king. The Hotel Biron, where Mothers de Charbonnel and Desmarquest, both timid women, were in charge, was in such danger that the chaplain thought it unsafe to leave any hosts in the tabernacle after Mass. The streets were full of shouting and the singing of the *Marseillaise*. The Sisters putting up the washing in the garden found themselves suddenly surrounded by flying bullets. They fled, but were safe. Nuns and children spent the day in the chapel. The government had fallen that day. Next day was hot and silent. The nuns were worn out by three sleepless nights, by the farewells to their departing students now mostly called for by their parents, by fear for their Superior in Conflans, and by patriotic grief for the royal family who had been so kind to them, and to whom several were personally attached.

At ten on the morning of the thirty-first, the little party from Conflans, all in secular dress, started back to Paris in a two-wheeled carriage so small that Mother de Constantin had to walk. She arrived first, and sent back two servants to meet the carriage. The driver had had to make detours on account of the barricades, and soon unwillingly took on another passenger, a genial drunk whose fuzzy shouts from the front seat had a patriotic ring. This obviously non-aristocratic fellow traveler guaranteed their respectability, as did their possession of a newspaper which the soldiers who stopped them at one point were anxious to see and gladly accepted as a passport. They had to alight at some distance from the house, and Mother Barat could not walk unaided, but the friendly drunk guided them, put up planks where the walking was bad, and even carried Mother Barat when it was too perilous to trust her crutches.

It was imperative that the novices be sent away from Paris. One of a group who went to Autun was a Belgian, Adèle Lehon, who had been a pupil a few years earlier in Amiens under Mother Prévost. In those days she had openly rebelled against all the customs of the house, and written back to her father that the nuns gave them shoe leather to eat. He had replied imperturbably that he congratulated her on her digestion. She stayed and was converted to a better frame of mind by Father Druilhet's retreat, and became the third Superior General of the Society.

Once the novices were disposed of, Mother Barat told her community that if the monarchy had fallen, the Church had not, and that they belonged to the Church. Though she had feared the dangers of prosperity, she did not fear persecution. On August tenth, she set out for Lyons, leaving in charge at the Hotel Biron Mother de Marbeuf, who had persuaded the King to help them buy it. One of those left with her was Sophie Dussaussoy, who at midnight Mass on Christmas Eve made her final vows at Versailles, where the reduced community had taken the few remaining children out of the still menacing atmosphere of Paris. The picture over the altar in the improvised chapel was the same that had hung before Mother Barat and her companions when they made their first offering thirty years before. There was another reminder of early days also, for the welfare of the group at Versailles was looked after by the Comtesse de la Rivière, who was none other than the Adèle Jugon who had revealed the eccentricities of Mademoiselle Loquet in Amiens, when the rest were too obedient to complain.

Although Madame de Genlis's scholar Louis-Philippe had become King on the last day of the year, unrest continued in the provinces. From Lyons Mother Barat sent nuns to the new house at Perpignan, where in February rioters broke in. One of the nuns found them in the study hall. She let the cover of a desk fall with a crash and cried sternly: "Gentlemen, are you Frenchmen?" and they hastily withdrew.

When leaving Paris, Mother Barat had written to Mother Audé in Louisiana: "We are going away, but where, I do not know." After stopping at Lyons and Autun, she went on to Chambéry, where a doctor, consulted about the increasing pain of her injured foot, advised her to stay a while at Aix and try what the waters there could do for it. It was only in October that she reached Switzerland, where the father of some Hotel

Biron alumnae, himself a peer of France who refused to recognize the new government, was taking pleasant refuge in a castle near Fribourg. The neighborhood was full of ecclesiastical and secular French dignitaries sitting out the revolutionary interval. There Mother Barat, with Mothers de Charbonnel and de Gramont, found affectionate welcome, and repaid her hosts' hospitality by sharing the family life and conversation with her usual simplicity and power of turning every subject naturally to God. As soon as the novices came from Lyons and Besançon (Adèle Lehon was of the company) to reorganize their life at a little rented house at Middes, Mother Barat joined them.

There was talk that Russia would attack France, and more than talk that the Swiss, alarmed at the invasion of so many French priests, were preparing to oust all religious. In December, Mother de Gramont returned to Paris. The Bishop of Fribourg advised Mother Barat to go to Turin or Chambéry if she wanted freedom to communicate with her other houses. Leaving Henriette Coppens in charge of the novices, she set out for Chambéry with Mother Desmarquest, but had another bad fall which so aggravated the now alarming state of her foot that she had to stop at Geneva. Finally, in great pain she went on to Chambéry, where the doctor ordered complete rest. She wrote to Mother Grosier that it was hard not to be able to do all that needed doing, but that, at a time when Christ was so outraged, it was good to suffer. At Niort, the crossroad Calvaries were being mutilated by the mobs, and she told Mother Emilie to honor a piece of one which had been tossed into the convent garden. Priests were in hiding again, religious ceremonies forbidden.

In Paris, Archbishop de Quélen's house was attacked, and he had to go into hiding. Two years later, Mother de Gramont, with more generosity than prudence, was to offer the Archbishop the use of a house on the Rue de Varenne property. This created an unusual situation, of which Mother Barat was uneasily aware, especially since it linked the Sacred Heart closely in the popular mind with the most intransigent opponent of the new regime. Even when not only other bishops but the Holy See itself recognized Louis-Philippe, Archbishop de Quélen, though polite, kept himself almost wholly aloof. Mother Barat, when she heard of Mother de Gramont's invitation, about which she had not been consulted, was appalled. The Archbishop's friends would come in crowds. The government would suspect the Society of plotting with him. Mother de Gramont, she urged, was to do all she could to prevent his accepting the invitation. But it was too late. He came, and was to stay nine years, during which his views on politics did not change.

Certainly Louis-Philippe was not popular with the Bourbon supporters. As Philippe Egalité's son, he was *persona non grata* with those who suspected that his father had precipitated the 1789 Revolution, and who knew he had abandoned his own social class and voted for the death of his brother, Louis XVI. However, once the new monarch had been accepted by the French people, there seemed little point in holding these understandable grudges, if the result was to make the work of the Church more difficult. Louis-Philippe was a skeptic, but careful to maintain good relations with the Holy See, and Gregory XVI permitted him to use the traditional title, "most Christian King." Mother Barat did her best to keep her Society clear of political alignments. She wrote explicit directions that the nuns in Paris were never to discuss politics in the parlor. She did tell Mother de Gramont not to contribute to a fund for raising a commemorative bust of Madame de Genlis, but gave as her excuse that the lady's principles had not been outstandingly Christian, and that anyway the King's name would undoubtedly head the list and mere nuns would not be noticed if they abstained.

The early months of 1831 were full of anxiety. She wrote: "I am a small edition of Job. Every mail brings news of disaster." She spent April and August 1831 at Aix in Provence, having been ordered to try the effect of the medicinal waters on her foot, but the waters did not help either, and it was a trial to be alone for weeks with only one companion. In June, she visited Grenoble for the first time since her miraculous recovery there eight years before. She never returned there without remembering the past and contrasting it with the feverish present. The town was still full of revolutionary fervor, and of troops to keep the fervor restrained, and one morning she watched the townspeople planting a tree of liberty. Mother Duchesne's cousin, Casimir Périer, with whom Philippine had studied mathematics when she was a girl and who always kept his affection for her, was high in the councils of the new national government, and though anti-clerical and skeptical like his confreres, was much more sane and moderate than most. He did predict the swift disappearance of Christianity, but did not try to hasten it.

During her second stay at Aix, she had the opportunity to consult Archbishop Lambruschini about her situation. She was supposed to go to Rome to arrange for the opening of a noviti-

ate there. She was also supposed to go back to Switzerland to
open the new house at Montet where the general novitiate was
to be transferred. But rumors of war, and the approach of the
cholera epidemic, and the continuing pain of her infirmity all
kept her in indecision. She was eating almost nothing, and at
Chambéry used to give her breakfast away through the window
to the altar boy, who had managed to get from her many other
small provisions before he was banished by the treasurer. In
spite of all her worries, she was able to write a gay letter to
Mother de Gramont saying that her Eugénie must have had a
fever when she wrote last, she had scolded her superior so
much. "It's my fault that I'm ill. It's my fault that I can't walk.
Soon it will be my fault if the cholera comes!"

By the middle of September, though no better, she had gone
to Montet to inaugurate a novitiate which, like the first novice-
ship in Poitiers, left the Society of the Sacred Heart most idyllic and austere memories. It was a small house in an enormous
setting, with the Alps on the horizon and pine woods all about.
There Henriette Coppens, a frank, forceful woman, was Superior and Mistress of Novices, and brought up her young nuns
severely but happily. Here, within a few years, were brought
up together to religious maturity Josephine Goetz, the Alsatian
who succeeded Mother Barat as Superior General, and Pauline
de St. André, daughter of a noble but latterly dissipated family,
who entered the Society as a coadjutrix Sister, and died very
young and very holy.

Seeing everything well in Mother Coppens' firm control,
Mother Barat, still in a semi-crippled state, went to Besançon,
and from there to Paris, for the first time in fifteen months, and
in November set out again for Lyons on the way to Rome. On

the Lyons coach trip, she had to stop twice, once when the coach broke down, and once when they were warned about food riots in Lyons. How difficult traveling was for her can be guessed from a note sent to Mother de Gramont on this second stop, saying that any opportunity to rest was welcome, and that she dreaded the interminable journey to Rome. Besides, what could she do there?

Everyone gave her different advice about going to Rome. She must rest at least a few weeks. She must take care of her injured foot, and of a new injury to her knee. She wrote to Father Rozaven in Rome, and announced that if he advised her to go, she would, no matter what anyone said. Father Rozaven told her not to come just yet, and she stayed in France, visiting her houses, and pursued by wild reports on the state of the world. Prophecies, she said, did not worry her. They deceived the credulous, but "your Mother is quite satisfied with the *Credo*."

While she was at Mother Geoffroy's Rue Boissac in Lyons, she suggested the formation of a Sodality of the Children of Mary from among the alumnae and women friends of the Society. The rules were written by Father Druilhet, who had collaborated with Father Varin on the Society's constitutions, and whose niece, Mother Lhuillier, was director of the Sodality. As he worded it, the Sodality was to help women living in the world to carry out the duties of their state in life, and devote themselves to prayer and good works, under the guidance of the Immaculate Mother of God. In February 1832, on what was later to be the Feast of Our Lady of Lourdes (though Bernadette Soubirous was not yet born) the first members consecrated themselves to Mary under the title of her Immaculate Conception.

Mother Barat went on to Avignon and then to Perpignan, where she heard that the cholera was raging in Paris. In an agony of indecision, she wrote to Mother de Gramont and suggested that as an intercessory offering the Society there take in some poor children orphaned by the epidemic. The Paris house was spared, though thousands died. Mother Duchesne's cousin, Casimir Périer, was one of them. Mother Barat wrote sympathetically to Philippine, saying Casimir had been their hope, for "at least," she remarked, "he had a good head." Meanwhile, in Provence, she was making a new foundation at Aix, and feeling stronger in the mild southern winter.

In May, Mother de Limminghe came to take her to Turin. They went by way of Nice to avoid quarantine regulations. On the road, they were held up by police on the suspicion that Mother de Limminghe, the most unworldly of women, was the Duchess of Berry, who, at the Hotel Biron, had had such hope for the future, and who was now an active agitator for the restoration of the Bourbon dynasty. Mother Barat, though exhausted, refused to go on until Mother de Limminghe's harmless identity had been established. She went to the police station, where the sergeant was courteously distressed to hear she had not eaten, and offered her two eggs. In return she presented him with two bottles of wine someone had given them as a gift for the journey. At midnight, they were allowed to proceed, and an hour later in Nice the carriage—as carriages had a way of doing—broke down.

At Turin there was now a school for poor children as well as for countesses. There, whether through the prayers of the children, rich and poor, or through the skill of the doctor—he was himself inclined to give the credit to the prayers—the miracle happened. Her foot was cured at last, and three years of helplessness were behind her. At a country property belonging to the house, she made her retreat, and wrote to Henriette Grosier: "More and more every day I feel that the habit of prayer is absolutely necessary to us." But for her, it had to be mostly, now, prayer in the midst of action, except for intervals of illness. She had a month of such illness in Turin, and some quiet hours to look back over the past year, in which her dear, volatile Chastaignier had died, as had Lydia Chobelet, so that now both the donors of the house at Poitiers were gone ahead of her to heaven. She wrote to Henriette Grosier that she was more than fifty years of age, and that the half-century had gone like a dream.

CHAPTER ELEVEN

1832–1839

Italy and Novices

From Turin, in August, Mother Barat wrote a letter to the whole Society, pointed out how they had been preserved so far from the cholera which was ravaging Europe, predicted that further troubles lay ahead, and asked prayers to avert them. She announced she would be in Rome in October. Before leaving Turin, however, she told Mother de Limminghe that she wished to place herself under her obedience in everything concerning her spiritual life. This would give her the opportunity, rare for one in her position of constant command, to obey in detail. Mother Barat's chief French biographer says she chose Mother de Limminghe because the two had similar spiritual attractions. It is perhaps more probable that she chose her because she had a quite different temperament, and therefore the obedience required would be more onerous. Mother de Limminghe, though she loved God passionately and served Him faithfully, was a melancholy, tense woman with little humor or sense of proportion.

On the way to Rome with Mother de Limminghe, Mother Barat accidentally burned her recently cured foot, which was so inflamed by the time she reached the Trinità dei Monti that she had to be put to bed. Pope Gregory XVI called unannounced four days later, and insisted on coming to her room, where she was by then sitting up in a chair. She tried to kneel, but he refused to allow it. His comment was: "How young she is!" They had a talk about the establishing of a novitiate, which he had approved. She had largely forgotten her Italian since the days when Father Louis had allowed her to learn modern languages as recreation from sterner studies, but the Pope helped her over the harder spots, told her she must come to the Vatican when she was better, and departed after embarrassing her by the remark that the Society was not only useful and edifying, but very well governed.

Almost a year before, in mid-winter, timid Mother Desmarquest had brought four novices from Switzerland to begin the Italian novitiate. One was Adèle Lehon for whom it was her fourth house of novitiate. They had wild adventures on the snowy way down the mountains, and waited at Turin before proceeding to Rome, where they arrived at the Trinità at the end of April. In November, Mother Barat was writing to Mother de Gramont about the monastery of Santa Rufina, in the poor Trastevere section beyond the Tiber, where the novitiate was to be placed.

The next week, she added, they were to call on Mothers Baudemont and Copina. A week later, she reported on this visit, which took place at the convent of St. Denis. The two nuns, she reported, had aged very much, and were suffering, but courageously. The house was pitiable. St. Estève had completely abandoned them, and they had well expiated any fault they might have committed by separating from the Society. A few weeks later, Mother Baudemont wrote, calling her "kind mother and friend," saying she kept for Mother Barat "a tender affection in our good Master," and praying God would bless her work. It was a happy end of the old misunderstanding, and a good example of how, as Mother Desmarquest said, "everyone in Rome was enchanted by her," and prejudices against the Society melted before her.

The Pope received her in audience, invited her to be present at his Mass, and on Holy Thursday sent to the Trinità a huge carp and some enormous eels. Mother Barat did not go sightseeing among the pagan remains in Rome. She wrote to her nephew that when she was young the memories now surrounding her in Rome would have lifted up her whole being, but "everything passes away." The city was only ruins. "Here you can stretch out your hand and touch the vanity of this world. God alone does not change and is great." She was more moved by the Christian monuments, but added: "Alas, looking at relics does not make you a saint! We must suffer."

Ten Italian postulants were waiting at the Trinità, under the guidance of Sister Adèle Lehon, still only a novice herself, who had picked up enough Italian to be understood. These Italians were so virtuous that Mother Barat told how one had fallen and broken her leg, but was disturbed only by the thought of the trouble she would be to others. If she liked her Italian novices, she intensely disliked Roman leisureliness. "In this country," she wrote, "business moves at a tortoise pace. It is killing for the French and needs the patience of a saint."

When the moment for the move finally came, there was some talk of a solemn procession through Rome from the Trinità to Santa Rufina. "Just fancy," she wrote to Henriette

Grosier, "all of us walking, apparently with candles in our hands, with a cardinal and his suite marching ahead of us. What a sight!" But she pointed out that the long distance between the two houses would make such a program a little wearisome, and the authorities reluctantly cancelled it. "How I thank God for it!" wrote Mother Barat. "I should have died of shame on the streets." So they went modestly, in small groups, with no parade.

On June 3, she left Rome, saying goodbye to Mother Desmarquest who, with only Adèle Lehon and the novices, was to open a free school for the excitable children of the neighborhood. It was the prospect of such a school that had particularly delighted Mother Barat. The parents were miserably poor and knew next to nothing about their religion, but were fiercely devoted to the Pope. In 1831, when someone tried to incite a rebellion against him, they had gone through Rome armed with knives, daggers and sticks, proclaiming their loyalty, met the Pope himself coming out of the Vatican, and removed the horses from his carriage to pull it themselves. So violent were their signs of affection that the Pope usually stayed away from the Trastevere, but he did come a few months after Mother Barat left, to see what was being done for the children of his unpredictable admirers.

On September 12 Mother Barat was in Paris and on the twenty-ninth, a Council was held at which the members discussed the training of the children. Father Loriquet came to help out in revising teaching methods, and Mother Barat told her nuns it was feeble-minded to cling to old methods through fear of innovation. Their job was to win souls. Nothing else mattered. Whatever within reason was needed to win souls by

education, they would do. Another decision was to suppress
the house of Ste. Marie d'en Haut, the beloved mountain of
Mother Duchesne's religious youth. Military buildings nearby
made the neighborhood undesirable.

Elections concluded the work of the Council. Elizabeth
Galitzin, the Russian princess, was chosen Secretary General,
and Mother Barat seems to have felt a little uneasy about this,
for she knew her Elizabeth, who was, after all, only a year or
two from her vows. She wrote drily that she hoped Elizabeth
would receive the news of her choice with humility, for the
job was more a chance to practise patience than an honor.
Mother Eugénie Audé was recalled from America, after fifteen
years, to be Assistant General. Her years in America had been
hard but fruitful. It was she who had had the success, Mother
Duchesne the contempt she prayed for. Eugénie had often
begged to be allowed to see her Mother General again. Mother
Duchesne was too austere to ask anything except that she be
removed from a position of authority where, she said, she
spoiled everything.

The next few years were a long succession of visits to new
foundations and routine business. On her travels, she did not
feel free merely to enjoy the temporary release from responsibility. The rules enjoined her to use every necessary contact
with people outside the convent as a chance to bring them to
God. Once she was alone in a small coach with two cart drivers,
who interrupted their talk of horses and markets to say:

"Look, Sister, people like you have no worries like ours."

"No worries!" she retorted. "Indeed I have worries, for
myself and for other people. So many of them never think

about the next life, yet it's going to last forever. How much do *you* think of heaven and hell?"

"Not much," they admitted. "Does that bother you? You must have a soft heart."

"I'm going to say my beads," she said. "While I do, you two think about this, and perhaps all of us who are together on this trip may be together again with God forever."

Impressed, they looked "Sister" Barat up when their trip was over, told her they had thought of her words, and promised to do what they could to stay out of hell and go to heaven.

Mother Audé, to her great sorrow, was not kept in Paris with her Superior General but sent as Superior to Marseilles, where another small community had joined the Society. Mother Barat wanted to go to her during 1835, but had another long illness at Lyons. From there she went to Jette-Saint-Pierre near Brussels, where another "noble" academy was to be opened—"with regret," she wrote, "for I prefer the poorest works." This house was, as a matter of fact, to be famous for its work for every class of society; and it is even more famous now, for her body lies in one of its chapels.

In Paris again, she separated the novices from the too handsome Hotel Biron and rented a new house for them on the Rue Monsieur. In the beginning of 1836, Mother de Gramont d'Aster, who had stood by her so staunchly against her daughters at Amiens, died a holy death at Le Mans. It was by now, as someone pointed out, becoming a hallmark of the Society that all its members died happily. But this did not lessen Mother Barat's regrets. Every year, she wrote, if she lived, she would lose more of her dearest friends. "It is true they die as they lived, like saints. What a lesson for us!" Meanwhile she went on visit-

ing houses (including, finally, Mother Audé's Marseilles), and
in August 1836 was back at the novitiate of Montet.

It was her third visit there in three years. The Montet novices
had none of the distractions inevitable in Paris. Life was completely rural. Once a visitor was horrified to recognize a noble
young lady of his acquaintance, now a postulant, still rather
fashionably dressed but caring, none too successfully, for the
pigs. The Jesuits had a house nearby, and Fathers Varin and
Druilhet came often to instruct the novices. Another Jesuit
whose name was to be closely connected with retreats at the
Sacred Heart in Paris knew the Society first at Montet. This was
Father Xavier de Ravignan, who had been a noted lawyer
before joining the Jesuits, and became one of the greatest
preachers of his day. Among the sixty nuns and novices Mother
Barat found at Montet were the two Nicolay sisters, of the
family who had sheltered her in Fribourg after the Revolution.
Three other sisters brought up at Montet in these years were
Emma, Eulalie and Elisa de Bouchaud, of whom all became
Superiors, and one, Eulalie, was to be Mistress of Novices in
Conflans and die there (too young, of course) in the odor of
sanctity.

Mother Barat wanted specially to see Pauline de St. André,
now Sister Elizabeth, who had entered as a coadjutrix Sister.
The Mother General had been wary of such a vocation, since
the girl had the ability to teach. Why, she asked her now, did
she not wish to use her gifts for God? Pauline replied that
Jesus Christ had glorified God by hiding His gifts, and that
she felt her vocation was to do the same. Mother Barat, whose
preference was for sweeping stairs rather than entertaining
dukes, understood, but prudently did not allow Pauline yet

to make her vows. She took her away to Chambéry and to Turin.

At Chambéry, the nuns told her the Queen often came to inspect the school she patronized. Mother Barat said that if Her
Majesty wanted to pass the Sacred Heart convent in review,
she could herself consider passing the Queen's troops in review!
At Turin, she watched Sister Elizabeth closely, "to see," as the
latter put it, "whether I am carried away by my imagination."
But she allowed her to make her vows.

In February 1836, she was back in Rome, where she needed
a new house for her novices. She found it on another hill, this
time the Janiculum. It was the Villa Lante, which had Rome
at its feet and the sky over its head. There she stayed fifteen
months with the novices in complete isolation from the world.
It was a peaceful year, with much prayer in it. She could write
to someone: "Ah, my daughters, how badly you are governed!
But fortunately Our Lord needs no one to do His work. The less
of man there is in it, the more there will be of God. If He wants
to use a mere nothing, He could hardly make a better choice
than of me." But that did not mean she was not firm and decided enough to send away an Italian novice of the name of
Colonna, whose ancestors had fought at Lepanto. Teresa talked
too much, and she had to go, no matter what her connections.

In the Spring of 1837 cholera was at Naples and coming
toward Rome. All summer, Mother Barat worried about her
daughters in the Trastevere, where the epidemic was at its
worst. She thought the Trinità, on its high hill, would be safe.
Mother de Limminghe felt responsible to the Society for the
Mother General's safety. For fear she might go to her daughters' help and so expose herself to the disease, she did not let
her know that it was the Trinità which the plague had struck,

that seven nuns there had died, that even the doctors had abandoned them, and that Father Rozaven had braved contagion to bring them the last sacraments. As might have been predicted, hearing the whole story at once was a shattering experience. "I thought I should die," she wrote, "as I heard one name after another. What nights I spend!" Worst of all must have been a sense of guilt at having lived so peacefully while her daughters needed her.

She was ill almost all that winter. Nevertheless she made arrangements for the Villa to take in cholera orphans, and tried to replace the nuns who had died, though there were other deaths of young nuns elsewhere about the same time, and it was hard to find anyone available. Spring made a paradise of the Villa Lante, but she said it was not landscape that interested her. She left Rome in May, still unwell, and went slowly, by way of the houses in Piedmont and Savoy, to Lyons, where she was too weak to go on. It was only at the end of August, 1838, that she reached Paris and went at once to the new novitiate on the Rue Monsieur.

Although always concerned that there should be sufficient laborers for the whitening harvest, she forbade her daughters to make any advances to their pupils about vocations. Only by their example and their happiness were they allowed to attract others, and she scolded Marie de la Croix, the fearful young nun of the Amiens crisis, now a Superior, for talking too much about vocations. If the pupils joined orders other than the Sacred Heart, she was equally happy. Once one of her religious told her she had wanted to enter Carmel but could not because she had not the dowry required. Mother Barat provided the dowry and sent her off to follow her first attraction. Always she stressed that the vocation to the Sacred Heart was not a vocation to a completely active life. "If we do not lead a contemplative life as well, the other will soon be a ghost, a body without a soul." She asked God specially to send her novices who loved prayer. It was this that mattered, not gifts or fortune. Once, she admitted, she had yielded to a natural desire to have in the Society a person who had fortune, rank, education, talent. But she soon became a cross to others, and eventually left.

The Mistress of Novices at Rue Monsieur was Eulalie de Bouchaud, a young woman of many talents and great holiness, with the single defect of being too timid. Mother Barat herself trained her, telling her to teach her novices to love God, work for souls and forget themselves. When she came to give instruction to the novices, she wanted them close around her. "Don't leave empty spaces. I don't like empty spaces. Man was not made for emptiness, but he will be empty unless he is filled with God." So that they would not be concerned only with themselves, she made them sew for the poor, and invited visitors like Bishop Bruté from America and Bishop Dupuch of Algiers, a former chaplain of the convent at Bordeaux, to remind them of the hardships of the missions.

Best of all, Father Varin, now sixty-eight years old, still came, not so much to preach as to sit down with the nuns and novices and chat with them and Mother Barat about the glories of the old days and the needs of the new. But Mother Barat would have no glories ascribed to her. The Society, she said, would be unlike others which had begun well and later declined. The beginnings of the Society had been so imperfect that only improvement was possible. When someone called her a pioneer in the work, she said the roughest stones were tossed into the foundations. If you remarked on her guidance of others, she replied that she was like a signpost showing the way but itself standing still, and added that when she wrote letters of direction she felt like a forger who, when he signed a bad check, was writing a warrant for his own arrest, or else like the crab in the fable, who criticized her daughter for not walking straight only to have the taunt thrown back on herself. Father Varin listened indulgently to these energetic and picturesque disavowals. It did not matter now how low an opinion Sophie Barat had of herself; it would never prevent her doing whatever needed to be done. He himself, like St. John in his old age, gave them perpetually the message of love of God and one another, or rather of Christ *in* one another.

During Lent of 1839, Father de Ravignan preached every week, but before the season had ended, Mother Barat had again gone away from Paris.

CHAPTER TWELVE

1839–1843
Paris or Rome?

During that Lent Mother Barat founded still another house, bringing the number to forty-one, with twenty-seven in France and fourteen outside. This constant growth was bound to bring changes; but some of the changes being suggested had nothing to do with the increase in the number of houses. Over-zealous members of Mother Barat's Council were forgetting that, as a Roman prelate pointed out, "the better is sometimes the enemy of the good." The changes were mainly three: to appoint Provincial Superiors to visit and supervise the houses, a task now too heavy a burden for any one person; to move the Mother House to Rome, and to adopt the rules of the Society of Jesus with almost no variation. Mother Barat thoroughly approved of the first, since no one could appreciate its necessity so much as she. The others she did not approve. The removal of the Mother House to Rome was advocated by Mother Galitzin and Mother de Limminghe, who were not French, by Mother de Charbonnel and Mother Grosier, who remembered the Revolution of 1830, and by all who specially feared the wavering politics of France or were specially at-

tached to the Holy See. Despite her attachment to the Holy
See, Mother Barat foresaw the storm of protest her departure
would raise among the French bishops, many of whom, before
1870, were jealous of their authority and resented "interference" from Rome. Aside from that, France was the cradle
of the Society and the chief field of its action. From there came
most of its vocations, and most of its financial support. The
government, which under Charles X had given approval to the
constitutions in 1827, might not care for a congregation whose
Superior General lived in Rome, and, since political affairs
were still highly unsettled, this was a serious consideration.

The matter of the constitutions, although it involved no
national or political complications, was intimately bound up
with the daily life of the Society. Mother Galitzin and Mother
de Limminghe, the strongest supporters of the changes, were
backed by such advisers as Fathers Barat, Loriquet and
Rozaven (who seems to have been influenced by his convert,
Mother Galitzin) and by some bishops. Mother Barat's terse
comment was that women could not be governed like men,
and that the Society was not called upon to prove that women
could become men, even, she added, in the nineteenth century, when men were becoming women. The Paris provincial
of the Jesuits objected that the rules of his Society were too hard
for women, and would demand of them what was beyond their
strength. Even Father Roothan, the Jesuit General, saw in the
attempt "fine dreams which would bring a sad awakening,"
warned that the Superior General's removal from France would
bring political repercussions and feared, with good reason, that
the Jesuits would be blamed for the whole affair.

Mother Barat, with her all-too-clear prevision of disagree-

ments ahead, was cautious in her invitations to the members
of her Council whom she summoned to Rome for their regular
meeting in June 1839. She asked them to keep the invitation
secret for a time. If, for some good reason, political or personal,
anyone could not come, she was to send word at once, and
give her opinion in writing on the subjects discussed. She even
used the words "forestalling a crisis." Mothers Deshayes,
Grosier and de Gramont could not come, and one of the Council
had died. Mothers Galitzin and Maillucheau were added, but
even so, there were only ten members instead of the usual
twelve at the deliberations at the Trinità, which lasted a month.

Nearly all the proposed changes were accepted, including the
suppression of Office in choir, a prolongation of the time required before making final vows, the granting after first vows
of the silver cross usually given only at final profession, and so
on through more than forty other major and minor amend-
ments. Mother Barat, seeing herself overruled, did not protest,
although as she later put it, she "made reasonable objections."
Mothers de Charbonnel, Desmarquest, Galitzin and de Limminghe were elected Assistants. The Pope granted an audience
at the end of the Council to all who had taken part in it, and
Mother Galitzin interpreted his gracious remarks about his
satisfaction with their labors as a general approval of the
measures taken. Then Mother Barat took them all to the Villa
Lante, where she read a consecration of the Society to Mary,
the Mother of Sorrows.

Her own attitude toward the changes was characteristic. She
refused to act until she was sure she had seen God's Will in the
concrete circumstances. His Will was never, she knew, some
prearrangement to which you had to resign yourself. It was

at every moment and in every situation a free, creative act by which, working with and through His creatures, He directed His creation toward ends only He foresaw. It was impossible to decide, without considering every demand of charity and prudence, what His Will was in any single case. She was not accustomed to leap into action without time to pray and to observe. In the extreme complexity of her present position, with wise and holy and well-intentioned people on both sides, she judged it better to wait, and was, as a result, condemned by both sides, each suspecting she was on the other. But the suffering that resulted she regarded as gain. What else was that Cross she was always recommending to her daughters as the best way to save souls? She refused to allow anyone but herself to be blamed for the way things had turned out. "If I was mistaken in acting as I did, at least I believed, as did many others, that I was working for our improvement." About her residence in Rome, she wrote to Mother de Gramont that she had consented to the change "only through duty, and not to refuse the Heart of Jesus the sacrifice that costs me most." When Henriette Grosier, who was very ill, said she was afraid Mother Barat's love for her might be lessened by their disagreement over the changes, she answered: "Our affection is based on the cornerstone which is Christ, and no human power can shake it."

To introduce such extensive changes into the constitutions would, she realized, require time. She wished to go in person to explain in each house what exactly the changes meant, and what were the reasons behind them. Her nuns would, she hoped, trust her, and this would make matters easier. But her advisers, especially Mothers de Limminghe and Galitzin, thought her kindness might degenerate into weakness, and insisted that a written announcement be drawn up and dispatched at once. Mother Barat did not hide from Mother Galitzin, who as Secretary General hastily and not too accurately composed the announcement, that she disliked her methods. The works of God, she reminded her, were not so precipitately done, nor could the rules of a religious congregation be remade at such speed.

Mother Galitzin's literary style was not calculated to soften the blow for those who did not agree with the new arrangements. In France, there was not only a cry of regret at losing Mother Barat, but a formal movement of protest, largely backed by Mother de Gramont, who had been named Provincial Superior of the North of France. The Superior General felt obliged to support the decisions of her Council. She herself believed the Holy Father wanted her to live in Rome, though she considered the time for such a move ill-chosen. The Pope was later to say he had never expressed any desire in the matter, but only satisfaction on hearing it had been amicably arranged. At the center of the storm, Mother Barat did what she could to pacify everyone. Wisely, kindly, disinterestedly, she gave information, urged submission, reproved indiscreet opposition.

At the insistence of Mother de Gramont, she agreed that the new regulations should be tested for a three year period only, after which a new Council meeting would decide whether they should be retained. Mother Galitzin, who had almost every talent except that of understanding and handling people, and who did not believe in preliminary try-outs, said impatiently of this concession that "her Assistants had tried in vain to persuade" Mother Barat to be firm, but could not succeed,

"so much did she fear to quench the smoking flax." Most of the
Society submitted to the trial suggested, but from outside
came strong objections. Father Varin declared that the Society
as he knew it no longer existed, and bitterly deplored the
dropping of the words "for the greater glory of the Sacred
Heart of Jesus," and the substitution of the Jesuit formula
"for the greater glory of God." By this switch they had, he
remarked in characteristically military language, abandoned
the flag of their regiment. He wrote to Mother Barat that this
was not the work of the Sacred Heart, and that if it went
through, it would be only honest to change the name of the
Society.

But the most powerful opponent was the Archbishop of
Paris. As Mother Barat had foreseen when Mother de Gramont
offered Archbishop de Quélen a residence on the Rue de
Varenne grounds, he had gradually come to take for granted
an authority over the Society to which he was not strictly
entitled. Pious and charitable as he was, he was reluctant to
have in his archdiocese a Society exempt from his control.
From her own house, and without consulting her, he wrote
in the autumn of 1839 to the French bishops in whose dioceses
the Society had convents, maintaining that the decisions of the
1839 Council were not within the jurisdiction of those who had
made them, and urging the bishops to send their objections, as
he had done, to the Pope. Five did so; others wrote directly to
Mother Barat, who reproached Mother de Gramont for not
having tried to prevent this move, or at least not warning her
that he intended to make it.

What afflicted her particularly was the publicity attracted
by this dramatic turn of events. Rumor was convinced that

some houses, including Paris, intended to break from the Society. This, she said, was untrue, but how painful it was to have everyone believe it. What had the Paris house to gain by such methods? Only scandal could result, and the withdrawal of God's blessing. The spirit of the Society was excellent, she insisted. If they were left to themselves, they could settle everything peacefully. After the three years' trial, they could discuss it all again. If the effects were as bad as some feared, it would not be too late to revert to the old regulations.

In December 1839, Archbishop de Quélen died. Mother Barat wrote to Mother de Gramont: "He is another saint in heaven, and a protector for us." She spoke tenderly of the special sorrow his death must be to Mother de Gramont, and asked solicitously about her health "after so much weariness, fear and anxiety." Mother de Gramont, who had not yet, after six months, put the new rules into operation, made the Archbishop's death a reason for delaying until she had the opinion of his successor. The successor was Denis Affre, whose views differed little from those of de Quélen, except that he had no personal reason for taking a mild stand with Mother Barat.

After his consecration in the following summer, Mother Barat, who was still in Rome, sent Mother Galitzin to him to explain the state of affairs. He seemed benevolent, but the soft word which turneth away wrath was not one of the languages Mother Galitzin spoke, and she failed completely to persuade Mother de Gramont to introduce the new decrees. So she set out for America to replace Mother Audé, and promulgate the decrees there. Leaving Mother Audé as Superior of the Trinità, Mother Barat herself finally came to Paris in September and made the dreaded changes, but slowly and gently.

The three years set for the trial she spent mostly in visiting her houses. It was during this interval that Pauline de St. André died on September 14, 1840, the feast of the Exaltation of the Holy Cross, after a very short religious life, full of suffering. In early 1842 Mother Barat returned to Rome, where she found Mother Audé also dying. She was with her at the end, and wrote of her: "She died as the blessed do, in resignation, trust and the sweetest peace."

Philippine Duchesne, who had been as old when she went to America as Eugénie Audé was when she died, was writing puzzled letters from Missouri about these confusing changes, so unlike what she remembered of the Society. But as a staunch admirer of the Jesuits, and their protecting godmother in the western wilderness, she could not protest the imitation of their rules.

In Rome, Mother Barat turned to her old friend Cardinal Lambruschini to ask direction. He said definitely that the forthcoming Council should be in France, and suggested Lyons, a half way place between Paris and Rome. Its Archbishop, de Bonald, had recently been named Cardinal, with the Trinità dei Monti as his titular church, and was a friend of the Society. Accordingly, she sent out notice of the time and place, inviting many more than the customary members, and urging that charity be the spring of every action taken.

No one was to come determined to hold to her own ideas. To the Rue de Varenne she wrote: "My sole thought now is to restore, by every means possible, peace and order to the Society." To Mother Galitzin she recommended prudence, moderation, peace. "If, from the beginning, all had acted so, what sorrows we should have been spared." But even these, she added, might yet prove useful to the Society. When someone else blamed Mother Galitzin, she replied: "There is no doubt that she acted in haste, but we were all in too much of a hurry. So I must defend her. Hadn't everyone the best of intentions?" Her skill in excusing is perhaps best shown in her reply to another dissident daughter in Paris: "I should be hurt by what you say if I could not distinguish your style from your heart."

She foresaw that the troubles were far from over, but if the Society could be saved, it would all be worth it. The date set for the Lyons Council was July 26, 1842. She arrived in Lyons, five days ahead of time, exhausted with the heat of the journey, and almost all those invited came shortly thereafter. With Mother Galitzin from America came a young nun named Aloysia Hardey, who had been brought up by Mother Audé at Grand Coteau and entered there in 1825. It was she who would soon become the master builder of the Society in America, and leave America at last to die in France, an Assistant General.

Mother de Gramont did not come. Instead came a letter from Archbishop Affre to Mother Barat saying categorically that no Council could be held, for he had jurisdiction over the Society and had not been consulted. He found her conduct, he said, inexplicable, but if his mildness had made her minimize his authority, he begged to correct her error. He had forbidden Mother de Gramont to attend. It was painful to him, he admitted, to see his good intentions toward the Society so ill received, but if she refused to obey him, she would find herself in a more painful position still. Thunderstruck, she sent him the sections of the Society's constitutions which proved it legal for her to call a Council without consulting him, and she wrote hastily to Rome to ask Cardinal Lambruschini's opinion.

Cardinal de Bonald, not wishing the Council held in his diocese under these delicate circumstances, advised her to delay it. In the stifling July heat, under pelting summer rain that brought no relief, Mother Barat prayed for light that did not come. From Paris other letters arrived telling her that Henriette Grosier was dying. To her old friend's sorrow and envy, she did return to God on July 28. Mother Barat had Father Barrelle give a retreat to her waiting nuns and then reluctantly sent them home. In Rome, eight cardinals in consultation decided Archbishop Affre was not within his rights, and wrote to tell him so. He accepted the decision, but added that it was regrettable that henceforward, since he had no authority over the Society, he could not intervene in its behalf if it had trouble with the government. Just then, as he must have known, the Minister in charge of religious affairs was preparing his own protest against the removal of the Mother General to Rome. The decrees approved by the government in 1827 had required her residence in Paris. If this were changed, the approval would be invalidated, and all the houses in France would be closed.

Mother Barat turned in desperation to another friend of the Society, Archbishop Mathieu of Besançon, a former confessor at the Rue de Varenne, who had been a lawyer before entering the priesthood, and whom Mother Barat had always hoped to see succeed Archbishop de Quélen. He agreed to take charge of the situation created by the man who had actually been named. From Besançon, she returned to Paris in November, and called on Archbishop Affre, who presented her dramatically with two documents for her signature. One was a petition to the Pope asking him to come to some understanding with the Archbishop of Paris about arranging a compromise between the 1839 and the 1827 constitutions. The other was a promise to the Archbishop himself that the Society would return to the 1827 constitutions, and that she would reside in Paris. She rejected the first and said she must think about the second. He told her she was free to save or ruin her Society. Strangely enough, the Archbishop had high personal regard for Mother Barat, and repeatedly observed to others that he much regretted the trouble she found herself in, for she was a very holy woman. He was sincerely convinced that what he required of her was necessary for the preservation of her Society.

Mother Galitzin, when she heard of these developments, wrote to say that, as she had suspected, the French were bringing undue pressure to bear on the Superior General, and that she would rather the Society be suppressed than not be Roman. Mother Barat answered firmly that she intended to stay in Paris, until the situation was clarified. If they wished, she said quietly, her Assistants could overrule her decision, remove her from office and appoint someone to replace her. There was nothing she wanted more. But in the meantime she begged them to come to Paris to consult with her. All evaded the invitation. Mother Galitzin wrote another of her imperious and accusing letters. Mother Barat replied: "Yes, dear Mother, the Society will judge us, and I am not afraid to give an account of my conduct. If the Society shares your opinion, I shall be easily consoled, for by losing its confidence I shall sooner and more easily obtain what I wish—to be *nothing*." Besides, she said, death could not be far off, for one did not suffer as she was suffering without danger to life.

In January 1843, Archbishop Mathieu went himself to Rome. He stayed seven weeks, and when allowed to decide the terms on which a decision would be made, asked that the *status quo ante* 1839 be revived, with some small modifications. The Pope confirmed this decision, and Mother Barat was informed. Juridically, the case was closed.

Mothers de Limminghe and Galitzin offered their resignation as Assistants, but Mother Barat replied affectionately that this would leave her with only two wheels to her cart, just when the affairs of the Society had to begin rolling. Mother Galitzin, always harder on herself than on anyone, asked leave to return to America to undo what she had done there. During Father Barrelle's retreat in Lyons, when the Society's position was most precarious, she had received permission to offer herself as a victim for the Society. God accepted the offering, for in December 1843, she died in Louisiana of yellow fever before having time to carry out her plans. Mother de Limminghe's resignation was accepted, and Mother Coppens was chosen to replace her.

There were to be many more trials from without in the twenty years left to Mother Barat, but there was never again, before or after her death, to be division in her Society. As in 1815, she was sure that the suffering had brought blessing. The Society had before its eyes an example it could hardly forget of how fatal was any attempt to act against authority, no matter how good the intention. God's work, once established, cannot be reshaped according to man's whim.

She herself had, through the agony of these years, reached

the sanctity toward which she had been moving since she first yielded to her brother's effort to make something of her. She had first really yielded when she came to Paris with him. By then, through the experience of sorrow, she had begun to see that no one makes his world. The world is constantly being made by Someone outside the world, Whose design is not to be guessed at yet, Whose ways—like her brother's—often hurt, but Whose infallible intention, unless we interfere, is our happiness through His Love. That was what her devotion to the Sacred Heart meant—a practical demonstration of her belief that every person and event in her life was a message of love. Her whole work was to decode this message and react as the situation of the moment demanded. If the years of her life up to now had seemed to have little external pattern, that was to the onlooker only, not to her. She did not always see what the pattern was, but she saw it was there, and she knew it was designed by a loving Heart incapable of error in the smallest calculation. During her trials she had often cried out and wished for death, but never refused whatever action the moment demanded. Nor had she buried herself in a fatalistic conviction that, if the will was God's, it would be done. She knew it would not be done except through her. When she said she was worth nothing, and that the doing was all God's, what she meant was that He could have done without her. But since He wished to use her, she recognized her obligation to offer Him the best possible tool. The process of her sanctity, as far as it depended on her, was a gradually spreading refusal to spoil what God wanted by substituting what she wanted.

Readers may still wonder, as some of her contemporaries loudly wondered, why she ever allowed her Counsellors to

make the 1839 changes in the constitution. The answer is simply that at the moment they had the authority to do so, and she was accustomed to see the Will of God in authority. She did not want the changes, but that was irrelevant. She trusted absolutely that God would do His work if she cooperated so far as she could see her duty. Her power of resistance, which stood up against the inclinations of her own heart and the battering of enemies who were good men, came from her conviction that God was working through her, and that she had to work with Him and to wait. The outcome overwhelmingly justified her. The process sanctified her. She once said to her novices: "Be forms of God. Like the sacramental species, be only appearances; let your substance be Jesus Christ." It was what she had now almost become.

CHAPTER THIRTEEN

1843–1850

War and Peace

At the height of the 1839 trouble, Mother Barat had remarked that, strange as it seemed, even saints have a hard time getting along together until they have passed through fire, that is, through the fire of the love of God or through the fire of Purgatory. She was herself all for staying out of Purgatory by suffering in this life. When peace was restored, her first thought was to begin her travels again, to close whatever wounds had been left by the four years of misunderstanding. The internal difficulties of the Society had not prevented its making foundations. In the United States, in Italy, in Algiers, in Ireland and England, houses were begun, usually in great poverty, occasionally without this highly desirable condition. One of Mother Barat's visits in 1844 took her for three weeks to England.

In the United States, where all the foundations had so far been along the Mississippi, one house was opened in New York and another in Canada, and the novitiate was transferred at least temporarily to Pennsylvania. Mother Duchesne, always conscious that she had not been a worldly success with the Americans, had been asking for years to be relieved of her position as Superior, which she had assumed so reluctantly when she left France. It was Mother Galitzin, never one to be sentimental about such things, who used her authority as Provincial to accept this retirement.

Mother Lucile Mathevon, who had gone to school at Grenoble and known Mother Duchesne there, describes how the fiery novice Mother Barat trained at Ste. Marie d'en Haut was completing the hidden way of her final perfection. She spoke of herself as a worn-out tool, a useless stick to be tossed in a corner. She slept in a damp little closet under the stairs, where she said she was more comfortable than anywhere else. "There are few canonized saints who have done as much as she," Mother Lucile wrote. The only thing she clung to was a longing to go convert the Indians, for whom she had originally come to America. Her mission to the American girls always seemed a mere distraction from her true mission to the savages. Besides, Father Peter de Smet, the great Jesuit missionary to the Indians, and a firm admirer of Philippine's, was always urging her to join him in working for them.

In July 1842, Mother Barat must have found it a restful change from her preoccupation with canonical disputes to be writing to her best-loved daughter, so long ago given, like everything else, to God: "Finally, you have reached those savage shores so long and ardently desired! May Jesus keep you and give you the means to do good there." But success, even in the Indian settlement of Sugar Creek, was not what God meant for her. She was ill and could not learn the Indian dialect (even her English was never very good), and after a year she returned to St. Charles to burn out there slowly for God. It was in the light of that burning that the Society in America walked, but few were conscious of the source of the light.

Nearer home, one of Mother Barat's favorite places was the new novitiate at Conflans, to which the Paris novices, under Eulalie de Bouchaud, had been transferred in 1842. Conflans remained for the rest of the century as nearly as possible that "central" novitiate which had seemed necessary twenty-five years before, but which was never, as the Society spread, to be completely practicable. From December 1842, when the chapel was blessed, Mother Barat made her residence there, sufficiently far from the Rue de Varenne, where her presence would then have caused some embarrassment. With the novices, she could forget the problems of administration which harassed these years. Nearby, the government was putting up military buildings, and Mother Barat, never able to see anyone close to her without offering temporal or spiritual help or both, arranged for the soldiers to make their first Communion in the convent chapel, fed them liberally, chatted with them, and even once took away with her to Paris, hidden in her carriage, a hothead who had punched an officer and had him pardoned for the heinous offense. Some years later, on a railway trip, she met the regiment which had then been stationed in Conflans. The soldiers welcomed her royally, piled up their sacks for her to sit on, and listened respectfully to a little talk she gave them while waiting for her train.

It was at Conflans that Mother Barat first met Marie Lataste, another of the saintly coadjutrix Sisters who have, in the course of the Society's history, demonstrated what a direct route to sanctity is the life of these religious, who do not teach or say Office, but otherwise have the same apostolic vocation as those

who do. Mother Barat envied their life, and when Pauline de
St. André had asked to follow it, thought she was taking the
easier way out by choosing a life of prayer and quiet work.
Marie Lataste was a country girl, though she had more education than girls in her position at that time had. For five years
before she asked to enter, she had apparently received extraordinary favors of intimacy with God, and revelations of high
doctrinal value. These were later to be published, but in a cor-
rected form which makes it difficult to know the original from
the corrections.

Mother Barat was reluctant to receive her. She was always
wary of revelations and an expert at unmasking them when
they were bogus. She had once written to sensible, matter-of-
fact Mother de Gramont: "I shall believe in revelations only
when *you* have them. If you have, let me know at once. Just
now, I am more incredulous than ever." Not that she doubted
the power of God. She had seen it in Mother Maillucheau, and
had some private experience. She simply wanted proof. Besides, she told one of her Superiors, she did not think God meant
this kind of thing for her daughters. "There are too few of us
simple and humble enough for such a way. I ask it for no one,
for it could be badly used." It was a loss, she admitted, but she
preferred humility, and thought the Society had reason to
cling to that virtue. Moreover she felt that this kind of favor was
not appropriate for nuns called to the active apostolic life.

Mother Barat accepted Marie but insisted that she be stren-
uously subjected to obedience and sacrifice. Under this treatment the girl flourished. She also, from the moment of her
entrance into religion, ceased to receive supernatural commu-
nications. Two years later she wrote that she was living a

humble, hidden life for God in Christ, and this was exactly what she wanted. Mother Barat's doubts vanished. After making her vows in 1846, Marie was sent to a new foundation at Rennes, and died there a year later, with such a reputation for holiness that, when the Society was driven out of France at the beginning of the twentieth century, her body was removed to Roehampton in England. It still lies in a chapel where rest also Father Varin and the two English Superior Generals, Reverend Mothers Mabel Digby and Janet Erskine Stuart—a chapel which was kept intact when World War II bombing destroyed the main body of the convent church.

In April of the year Marie entered at Conflans, Eulalie de Bouchaud died, and the day after, Antoinette de Gramont, Eugénie's less colorful younger sister, Superior at Le Mans. There was still, too, the recurring sorrow of losing the young nuns. Father Varin's niece, Aglaë, had died in 1841, and Father Druilhet's niece, Mother Lhuillier, in 1843. At Conflans, with Mother Barat, was Mother de Charbonnel, now almost completely blind, but teaching the novices many things, not least by example. She predicted that these novices would live through harder times than she herself had seen.

These times were not far off, but first Mother Barat enjoyed another of those idyllic intervals so rare in her life. A month after Mother de Bouchaud's death, she set out for Rome, slowly, by way of her southern houses. There was nothing idyllic about this, for she was ill most of the time. In January of the following year, she stopped at Genoa, where a new house had just been opened, by Armande de Causans, the pioneer of the Trinità dei Monti, and a young nun named Anna du Rousier, who was shortly to have more than her share of the hard times

Mother de Charbonnel had predicted. In Rome she went at once to her novices at the Villa Lante, and found among them an Irish postulant, Marie O'Mahony, who had been a pupil at Montet, and had come to Italy hoping, as so many Irish and English of those days vainly hoped, to be cured of tuberculosis. She died there in Mother Barat's arms. Many years later, Janet Erskine Stuart, when she was Superior General, wrote of seeing her grave in Rome, and thinking how strange it was to find her so far away from Roscrea, the Sacred Heart house in Tipperary where she had run about as a child.

Mother Barat spent the spring of 1845 at the Trinità dei Monti where another postulant not quite so young, Pauline Perdrau, was painting a fresco of Our Lady in the Temple as a young girl. She is shown sitting before an open door, with a book lying open on a sewing basket on the floor before her, a distaff on one side, and a single stalk of lilies in a tall vase on the other. This was to become the miraculous Madonna of the Lily, now known as Mater Admirabilis. In every house of the Sacred Heart on five continents there is a copy of the picture. Mary, in her pink dress with its laced bodice, and with her single curl (which Mother Barat pretended to find frivolous) escaping from her veil, presides at the end of some corridor in every Sacred Heart school, teaching the girls, who find in her a girl like themselves, that God may have great things in store for them, too, if they will take the time occasionally to shut out the earth, as she is doing behind her lowered eyelids, and think of something other than the apparently lovely world.

In May, word came from Bordeaux that Mother Geoffroy had died, at eighty-four, and that an artist called in to sketch her gave up, saying: "How can I? Her face grows younger every hour!" Mother Barat said of her: "We have lost our Moses who prayed on the mountain. Who will replace these pillars of the Society?" She devoted herself tirelessly in her last years to training those who would.

One of them, Pauline Perdrau, left an account of her trip that summer with Mother Barat from Rome through northern Italy. They left in June, with Mother de Limminghe, whom Mother Barat still loved and trusted despite the disagreements of recent years, and Mother Adèle Cahier, Mother Barat's secretary, who was eventually to write her life. At Assisi they met a whole community of Poor Clares to whom Mother Barat had made many gifts and who, since she could not come to them, went in a body to waylay her on the road. There followed a few hours of conversation, with a good meal for the poor Franciscans provided by Mother Barat, and a parting that came too soon. Through the long, hot summer days, the carriage lumbered on, with Mother Barat winning over and converting the driver, Georgino, and allowing herself to be distracted now and then by the view, especially along the Adriatic, where she strained her eyes to see whether she could glimpse the shores of Greece she had so loved in her "classical youth." "I was all fire and flame for Greece," she said, with its superb literature, and its battles in which the few, by mind and personal worth, vanquished the mob. She could laugh still, she told them, when she remembered how she agonized over Thermopylae and the Macedonian wars. This was how to present history to the young, she added, in a way that roused them, though not excessively, and made them feel themselves present at these great events. Eventually, by this method, they would come to

see the *sic transit gloria mundi,* and long for a world without
shadow or change.

There were the usual bad inns and worse meals and sleepless
nights, but Mother Barat had forty years of the same behind
her. At Parma, where they stopped, she refused to walk on a
red carpet which had been spread on the stairs joining the convent with the palace of their benefactress the duchess, and she
deplored the splendor of the monastery the nuns had been
given. There was nothing to do about it when such houses were
a gift, she admitted, perhaps recalling the regrettable splendors
of the Hotel Biron, but at least the nuns should be careful not
to build in the same way. At Turin, Mother du Rousier, who
had just become Superior, had to announce to her the news of
Father Barat's death two weeks before, in Paris, on the feast
of his patron, St. Aloysius Gonzaga. She asked to spend a day
alone before the Blessed Sacrament, praying for the brother
who had set her on the way she was so laboriously walking,
while he himself had had rather a peaceful, though a fero-
ciously mortified, life, teaching Hebrew and Scripture to young
Jesuits. Even in the 1839 affair he had been on the opposite
side from hers. But to give her trouble was always, with Mother
Barat, the best way to keep her affection.

After Turin there were farewells to be said to Georgino.
Mother Barat gave him a watch, and he left her crying: "There's
the kind of saint for me! I won't mind going to heaven if they're
all like *her!*" He turned back to Rome, remembering the little
walks they had had, she leaning on his arm and gravely discussing with him the none too promising state of his soul, while he
stoutly swore improvement for the future.

After stopping at Montet, now no longer a novitiate, where

Mother Maillucheau was Superior, they went on to Kientzheim in Alsace, where the Montet novices had been sent, and so eventually to Conflans, more than three months after the departure from Rome. There Mother Barat had a short space of quiet with the novices, with Mothers de Charbonnel and Desmarquest to recall the first days of the Society, and Father Varin to urge them to keep up the holy desires of their predecessors. To this time belongs the story of a novice dying of what seems to have been a brain tumor, whom Mother Barat cured by her touch, although she was careful to attribute the miracle to Saint Philomena.

At the Rue de Varenne, Mother de Gramont was dying, and Mother Barat went to devote herself to the care of this very dear, very virtuous daughter, who had caused her such sorrow. She called her "the little Mother," and defended her vigorously against those who accused her of letting the boarding school be worldly. She was, by all accounts, a most unworldly person, who always remembered the years in England when her exiled mother worked to support three children. Everything about her office was scrupulously poor. But she had been at the Hotel Biron for twenty-six years, and some of its gilding had, in the minds of the public, rubbed off on her. When Mother Barat came, she found her unable to leave her room and suffering terribly as the result of a heart attack brought on by staying day and night with the pupils during an epidemic of scarlet fever. But suffering had been almost her trade, and Mother Barat wrote that even she, who knew the little Mother so well, was astonished at her rapid stride in virtue these last years. As she had so long regretted the Amiens misunderstanding, so now again her main anxiety was that Mother Barat forgive her the misunderstandings of 1839. Her Mother General told her that she had not only forgiven but forgotten.

Her illness and death caused a furor in the fashionable St. Germain section of the city, and liveried coachmen left messages and inquiries all day at the crowded front door. After her death, her family did not think the funeral customary in the Society elaborate enough, and Mother Barat, without warning, heard strains of stringed instruments and voices of hired singers coming from the visitors' chapel. She said nothing, but afterward refused to see the family when they asked for her, and her point was not lost. To the community, she remarked that this was a sign of what Mother Eugénie had been combatting all these years, for it was only when she was dead that such things happened. She would never have permitted them.

But fashionable Paris also predicted that with Mother de Gramont's great name withdrawn, the school would swiftly decline. It did nothing of the sort. Mother Barat unobtrusively took over, changing small regulations about who would be received in the parlors and how often, and arranging that her nuns should use a back corridor so as not to encounter the visitors unless their duty required it. She also had what gilding was left painted over in gray, and she sold the marble fireplaces. She gave herself completely to a spiritual renewal among her daughters, and whatever reform was needed (as some reform is always needed) came from within. The school was still a cross-section of the world, and she strengthened the studies and taught her nuns to be loving mothers to all the children, who would later, she correctly predicted, call the nuns of the

Sacred Heart to open houses in the countries from which they came.

Soon the hard times Mother de Charbonnel had foreseen were upon them. Another revolution was brewing, which would in 1848 overthrow Louis-Philippe and in 1851 replace the Second Republic by the Empire of Louis Napoleon. As usual, there were violent anti-clerical manifestations, but fewer this time in France than elsewhere. Mother Barat, who made loyalty to the Holy See one of the major points of her teaching, was especially touched by the attacks on Pius IX. But her own Society was not spared. In Switzerland, Montet, with its precious memories, was lost. There as elsewhere it was the connection between the Society and the Jesuits that brought on many of the disasters.

In Italy, Mother Barat's nuns were called Jesuitesses, and parodied on the stages of theaters and in the press. The house at Turin was too closely linked with the government not to be one of the first to fall. Mother du Rousier dispersed her nuns among the other houses, and herself managed to reach Paris with some of them. For a time she took over the school at the Rue de Varenne, but the pupils did not think so highly of her as the Piedmontese pupils had, and Mother Barat had to make one of her rare punitive appearances before them, in which she spoke of Mother du Rousier's value and then told them that she was being taken from them. She was sent first to the United States to make a visitation, and spent the rest of her life founding houses in South America in the midst of hair-raising adventures, which must have made the attacks of Piedmontese rebels seem tame.

Mother Barat's power to frighten and melt the cocky little

aristocrats of her school when others—even those who had
faced revolutionaries—could not, shows what power lay behind her customary mildness. Mother Perdrau, who was at the
Rue de Varenne during the 1848 revolution, has left memoirs
of it which bear out this power. It came largely from her insight into people. Once a group of ruffians arrived to announce
that they intended to tear up the paved front courtyard and
plant one of those trees of liberty to which French republicans
were addicted. The portress, a former missionary to the United
States, stalled them off until she could get directives from
Mother Barat. The directives were simple. These good men, she
said, were to be asked in and given some wine and other re-
freshments. Meanwhile, the convent gardeners would be glad
to dig up a nice tree and help them replant it in the courtyard.
Shortly thereafter, the fierce band departed refreshed, leaving
behind them merely a transplanted mulberry tree.

She could be just as strong and often less diplomatic with
her own nuns. At the worst of the riots, she had sent away her
young nuns who had not yet made their final vows, to stay with
their families, where they would be safer, until they were called
back. Mother Perdrau, who was one of them, went but could
not bear the thought of staying overnight out of her convent,
and so, since things seemed quieter, came back the same evening. Mother Barat refused to see her, and sent word that she
was to go home at once and stay there until sent for.

Gradually all the handsome houses in Piedmont were closed.
At Genoa, Armande de Causans had to abandon her house and
get her nuns out of Italy as best she could. Mother Barat was
kept at the front door of the Hotel Biron welcoming pitiful
bands of fugitives, and resettling them elsewhere, many of

them, like Mother du Rousier, on missions outside Europe. Meanwhile, at the Rue de Varenne, the nuns of the house set up their beds in attics and at the end of corridors, to make space for the tired, frightened refugees, who arrived in attire that was afterward contributed to the costume collection for the school plays.

But the Paris house itself was unmolested, thanks to Mother Barat's charity. She fed the hungry in the famines which swept the city, until the government made her stop for fear the mobs who came might cause trouble to others besides the nuns. A wounded man brought into the courtyard by his friends during a riot was cared for by the best doctor in Paris, persuaded to go to the sacraments, and sent away cured, with food and new clothes. In June 1848, Archbishop Affre was shot on the barricades as he tried to conciliate the men who were being forced into the army. On his deathbed, he sent a message to Mother Barat, asking pardon for any pain he had caused her. She spoke of him as a good shepherd who had died defending his sheep, and asked for a relic of "this latest saint."

But if she was calm and could control the situation, she still suffered intensely at the thought of the insults offered to God through the attacks on the Church, and she could not forgive herself for doing so little to repair them. She wrote to Mother Thérèse Maillucheau: "Since the past is no longer in our power, we can at least throw ourselves on the divine mercy, and try in the evening of our lives to set our guttering torch ablaze again." Thérèse was no longer a Superior, and her old friend envied her. She could write only rarely, but reminded her that one of her few slight virtues was that of being faithful to her friends.

As soon as things quieted down a little, she completed a foundation at Marmoutiers. The ancient monastery of St. Martin became one of her favorite places of retreat, and there, a year later, Geneviève Deshayes died at eighty-three. Mother Barat was expecting another loss even more painful. Father Varin, who was also over eighty, and very frail, reminded the novices at Conflans: "How well off we shall be in heaven." He told them that when they died, they could all say to God: "You Who gave me such good companions when I was on earth will surely not put me in worse company now?" and he always added his watchword: "Courage and confidence!" He died in April, 1850, and went to join the good company he had so effectively helped to heaven.

CHAPTER FOURTEEN

1850–1865

Paris

To describe the last years which separated Mother Barat from
the same good company is to show what seems to us an already
finished work being gradually polished to a brilliance too great
to be quite caught by human eyes. There were more foundations, and more revolutions, and more deaths, while she for the
most part lived in Paris, gathering the children about her and
visiting the novices. She was keenly interested in the never-
ending question of freedom of religious teaching, and kept in
touch with those most concerned in promoting it. She appreciated the writings of Félix Dupanloup, and shared his notion
that education was a process of mental development rather
than an accumulation of facts in the memory.

Nevertheless, she had no scorn for facts. In 1833 she had
written to Mother Aimée d'Avenas that the Society needed
learned saints. She was writing from Rome, and added that in
the novitiate there, a few had holiness, but absolutely none
had learning, though only the combination of holiness and
learning would give perfection to their work. In her rule she
did warn her daughters against the "vain pretentiousness of a

proud age," in such matters, but this was the age of ladies like
Madame de Genlis. It was the salon type she seems to have
had in mind when she recommended, as an antidote, "the
humble and prudent discretion which modesty prescribes in
such matters to persons of their sex." Mother d'Avenas, one of
those fortunate girls who shared their brothers' education, was
a classicist and historian. When she entered the Paris novitiate,
she so missed her intellectual milieu that she left, only to return later and become head of the school at the Rue de Varenne,
and organizer of the studies of the young nuns. When Father
Dupanloup was made Bishop of Orléans, he at once asked for
a house of the Sacred Heart in his diocese. Mother Barat said
such a learned Bishop should have a literate Superior for his
foundation, and sent him Mother d'Avenas.

It was during the last few years of her life that she was particularly preoccupied with improving the studies of the nuns
and the pupils, and her letters are full of advice about the
school. Several are to her niece, Sophie Dussaussoy, who was
usually in charge of the studies. In 1863, she writes to her at
Niort that she must try to make the children happy, not only
by improving their spiritual life but by giving them a love of
work and of study so far as they are capable of it, and she adds
that she has always noticed how much more sound is the spiritual life of the pupils when they are being taught to work
hard, for then their religion does not exist in some kind of pious
vacuum.

A rather surprising group of letters are those to Mother Con-
stance Bonaparte about the education of two of her nieces.
Constance was the daughter of Lucien Bonaparte, brother of
Napoleon I. She had the family temperament—stubborn, vio-

lent, intractable, and when her parents, who were living in Italy, wanted to send her to the school at the Trinità, she at first gave in very reluctantly, but turned her strong will in the direction of good, entered the Society, and devoted herself to the conversion of her family. She was a first cousin of Napoleon III, and his wife, the Empress Eugénie, was interested in her and in the two nieces she was educating. Eugénie had been a close friend of Mabel Digby, an English girl who entered the Society in Pau and was to become its fifth Superior General.

In 1855, Mother Barat wrote to Mother Constance at Roehampton in England, advising her to fortify her nieces against "the glamor of the grandeur and wealth which will be offered them." She also asks after Mother Constance's nephew, who has become a priest, and who was later to be a cardinal. For both nieces and nephews, she recommends that the aunt sanctify herself by stooping, for the love of God, to all the irritating details of a teacher's life: being watchful and tidy, and foreseeing all that must be done to make her work solid and lasting. It is amusing to find the barrel maker's daughter from Joigny discussing with Napoleon's niece what steps she is to take about her royal rights of inheritance. In 1863, she writes to her that all the world wants now is to keep going, as a train does on rails without touching solid ground. Everything is sensation and excitement; everything is blown up and empty, like the fashionable crinolines.

At the same time that she was discussing the education of princesses, she could write to thank Mother d'Avenas for a gift of peaches, and to thank her niece Sophie for some cheese, adding that the cheese was usually too highly spiced and irritated her throat, so that it was hardly worthwhile to send it.

To someone else she suggested that if she sent pears again she should wrap them more carefully lest they be bruised, and that anyway, since she could get pears nearer home, it was not worth the expense of sending them. She had always spoken unselfconsciously about the state of her health when she thought people were worrying about it, and she continued to explain her handwriting by the pain in her thumb or the rheumatic state of her arm. To Mother Eveline Levêque, an American born nun who cared for her at the Mother House in the last days, she sent thanks for a "muff" made to keep the cold from her stiff arm, and for a writing folder which is almost too handsome to use—but how can she scold her for making something better than she had been asked to make?

In 1851 there was another trip to Rome, to ask again that she be given Mother Provincials to help her in the government of the sixty-five houses of the Society. This permission, refused at first, was given when Pius IX learned how pained she was by the refusal. But the Provincials were to be called Vicars instead, to show their close union with and subordination to the Mother General.

In 1852, Mother Duchesne died at St. Charles in Missouri. The friendship between her and her Mother General had survived thirty-four years of separation. For the last years, since the abortive mission to the Indians, she had been living in complete obscurity and in as much mortification as she could persuade her Superiors to allow her. One of her worst trials during this time occurred in a period of several years before 1847 when, for some reason never completely explained, the letters sent to her by Mother Barat did not reach her. Receiving no reply to her own letters, the valiant missionary, who always passionately loved France and her friends there, had the final sacrifice of believing that the Mother General was no longer interested enough to answer her. This was quite understandable, she thought, and stopped writing. But Mother Barat was so puzzled by this silence that, when in 1847 Mother Amélie Jouve, Philippine's niece and Aloysia's sister, went to Canada, Mother Barat sent her specially to St. Charles to have news of this friend of now very distant days, of whom she said the highest thing she could say: that she "understood the value of souls and never drew back before any obstacle" when called to help them. Philippine would be glad to know, too, that the year before, the Society had acquired a house at Montfleury just outside Grenoble and overlooking the Isère, near to Ste. Marie d'en Haut.

After this, the letters began again. In August 1852, Philippine wrote with her usual matter-of-factness: "It is quite probable that this is the last time I shall write to you. Yesterday I received the last sacraments." She did not know when the end would come, and thought that perhaps God might make her wait still for the happiness of seeing Him. He made her wait until November of that year. The very night of her death, this fervent disciple of Louis Barat told her Superior, who had been her novice, and who insisted on lighting a fire in the dying nun's cold room, that it would be better for her to say an Our Father and a Hail Mary for her soul than to be fussing about her body, which certainly had had no fussing from its owner. She was eighty-four years old, and had come to begin a new life on the American mission when she was almost fifty. Just before her death, Mother du Rousier, who had been a child at Poitiers in 1818 when Philippine had stopped there on her way to America and spoken to the school, saw her again, and it was the Duchesne spirit which, a year later, she carried with her to her work in South America.

In 1856, both Emilie Giraud, Mother Duchesne's first novice, and Mother de Charbonnel died, and in the following year, Thérèse Maillucheau. Mother de Charbonnel was her scrupulously honest self to the end. When, at her deathbed, the priest asked whether she loved God with her whole heart, she answered: "I want to." Mother Barat, who did not "like empty spaces around her," had lost all her first companions, but she could say: "And yet I am not alone, for the Father is with me." Up to the end, she was harried by the business of government, but she followed the advice she gave to others: "Get used to acting in the sight of God by a pure intention of acting for Him and pleasing Him. This takes neither time nor effort. One look, one lifting of the soul is enough. The important thing is to acquire the habit." She had very early acquired it, and it grew with the years.

She managed in the midst of incessant occupations to find an astonishing amount of time for prayer. What she could not find during the day, she made up during her more-often-than-not sleepless nights. Many, including her doctors, tried to persuade her to "distract herself from God," so that she could sleep, but she would not hear of this. Her power of constant prayer had been bought by long self-control, and by suffering gladly endured; not only control of the body and physical suffering, but more important, control of the imagination and the mind, suffering of the soul. Anyone who practised this made herself an expert at hearing and answering the inspirations of the Holy Spirit, and then all the virtues followed. She liked to say that this was the holiness of the earliest Religious of the Sacred Heart, those great souls now all enjoying their reward. They had prayed always and worked always, their prayer leading them to work, and their work full of the spirit of prayer.

But though prayer and work were combined, she knew that the Mother House of the Society should be a place unlike the Hotel Biron, which was, she said, like an inn at the time of a fair. She tried twice to establish a Mother House in houses on the Rue St. Jacques and the Rue Cassini, but neither succeeded, and in 1858 she moved to her final home, a building erected on the grounds of the Hotel Biron, but at the far end from the school, so that the work of the Mother General and her Assistants, and the quiet of the young nuns returned for a brief further time of training before their final vows, might not be disturbed. From here, she paid long-looked-forward-to visits to the school, or invited the youngest children to come to see her at the Mother House, where they were given elaborate snacks, and talks about the good God and the little Jesus. She had never lost her interest in the school and its smallest details: the tiny rich girl who wept on being put into a plain pinafore and sent to bed in a little curtained dormitory alcove, not because she disliked either, but because she thought her family had suddenly become poor; the father who brought his little girl to the Sacred Heart and said caustically, in front of the child's expensively furbelowed mother, that the mother was too taken up with her social life to care for her child; the line of little girls who one by one silently licked the sugar off the cakes unwisely left at the entrance door of the school dining room where the ranks passed. Nothing was too small for her interest, her laughter, her advice.

She never lost her vivacity. Once at the Mother House, where a young nun was portress, she rang a little bell, the usual signal for the portress to come to her. The young nun was hurrying to do so when Mother Desmarquest, always a calm and measured person, heard her from the next landing and came out to tell her not to rush in this unseemly fashion. She obediently slowed up; but no sooner was Mother Desmarquest's door closed than Mother Barat's opened, and the Mother General came out saying: "Didn't you hear me ring? Come quickly!" A priest who watched this little comedy asked the portress when she returned: "Which do you obey?" She said: "Both, one after the other."

Her speech was full of picturesque figures: "Don't bargain with Christ. If He asks for a sample, give Him the whole piece." "Before lighting the fire of the love of God, you have to clean the soot of self-love out of the chimney." "The slightest infidelity is like a stitch dropped in knitting. The whole thing unravels." There was even such intensity in her way of speaking that she often lost her voice, and then she would remark: "My mother used to tell me: 'The only good thing about you is your tongue.' Now I haven't even that."

But this liveliness must not make us forget that here was a woman who spent months in bed almost every year with some sort of respiratory infection always accompanied by fever. She suffered from rheumatism, for which the primitive remedy suggested by even the best doctor in Paris was to rub her limbs with a hot iron, and this heroic treatment was administered by a nun with no skill or gentleness, who habitually left burns on her patient's skin. Nevertheless, she devoted up to seven hours every day to an enormous correspondence, to which she replied with her own hand, pushing her goose quill with fingers stiff with pain, often unable to reread what she had written, for one eye had very dim sight, and the other, when she was unwell, watered so badly that she was almost blind. Her own suffering made her tender to that of others. She spent hours with the sick, cared for them herself when she could, supervised their care minutely when she could not, even went up to an attic room on her knees to visit a sick novice when she could not use her own legs.

In 1859 revolution again swept Italy, and though houses of the Society again fell in the struggle, Mother Barat was more distressed by insults to the Holy See than by any loss of her own. When the papal troops were routed at Castelfidardo, near the Sacred Heart house at Loretto, the wounded took refuge in the convent; but soon Loretto had to be closed, as well as the house at Perugia, founded at the request of Cardinal Pecci, who was to become Leo XIII. Mother Adèle Lehon, who had once accused the Amiens nuns of feeding her shoe leather, was now the Superior Vicar of Italy, and had to supervise the closing of these houses and provide for the expelled nuns. Mother Barat wrote to her that such outbreaks resembled the disorders pointed out by Christ as signs of the approaching end of the world. These signs must only make the nuns of the Sacred Heart more eager to sanctify themselves and others. Crimes flooded the earth, and the Divine Victim, she said, needed other victims to help Him. She always had sufferings of her own to offer. The American Civil War, which placed several of her houses in the South in peril, was a continual source of anxiety, and in 1863, Mother Henriette Coppens died.

In 1864, she called her last Council. She was eighty-four

years old, but they would not allow her to resign. They did, however, give her Mother Goetz as her Vicar General to take from her all she could of the labor and the anxiety. Her advice to her Vicar General explained her own secret of governing. She told her to become more and more convinced that she could do nothing of herself, and that when she was completely convinced, God would act through her. "The less we have, the more we can hope for." The Council lasted a month. The Society now counted eighty-six houses (though many others had been closed) and three thousand five hundred nuns, all since that day sixty-five years ago, when Sophie Barat offered the nothing she thought herself to be as a weak tool for God to work with. The Council closed the day before July 22, Mother Barat's name day. She had, this year, the kind of feast present she liked best. An alumna of the Paris house had lost all her money, and her husband, too ill to support his family, and embittered by his misfortunes, had given up the practice of religion. When the wife decided to ask for help, he sneered that Mother Barat was too much the great lady to bother with down-and-outs like them. The great lady's swift response, pouring out on them all she could afford or get others to contribute, brought him back to God, and on the feast day the wife came to tell her benefactress that her husband had that day returned to the sacraments.

The winter of 1864 to 1865 found her ill and tired. The fire was going out slowly. She was almost all soul and no body, and she talked of nothing but the love of God. In spring, she was a little better. They wrote that the last of the old building at Amiens was being torn down, and though she regretted this, she said that if the nuns remembered the virtues practised

there, the walls themselves did not matter. In March she wrote
to her priest nephew: "I am near—my weakness tells me very
near—the end." Her long life, she said, seemed to have passed
like a dream, but it was good to know she had fought for and
loved and tried to imitate Jesus meek and humble. She did not
think she had succeeded very well, but hoped for mercy. On
the ninth of May, she was able to see some of the children,
under the cedar tree in the garden, gave them candy, and told
them never to offend God, for otherwise, how could they see
Jesus and His Mother in heaven? "And you love them both,
don't you?" She was happy about the school and the nuns.
"Everything is going well," she wrote contentedly to Mother
Prévost, who was Superior at the Hotel Biron, down the long
walk at the end of the Rue de Varenne.

On the twenty-first of May, the Sunday before the Ascension,
she went to the young nuns and said: "I was eager to come to
you today, for on Thursday we are going to heaven. We must
see each other a while before that." As always, she called them
close to her, so as not to leave empty spaces. She read them
letters from some little boys at Marmoutiers. One told her: "I
am praying to God that you may live a long time." She shook
her head over this, and preferred one which said: "I am asking
to go and be with you in heaven." As she was going back to
her room, she met some of the nuns and told them to be very
humble, for if this rung were missing from their ladder, they
would never reach heaven. That day she wrote an eight-page
letter to one of her Superiors, and went to Benediction with
the children who were beginning their retreat before First
Communion.

Next morning, after she had been to Mass and Communion,

just as she began to read her usual pile of letters, she had a stroke. She lingered until Thursday, the feast of the Ascension. She gave slight signs of being conscious most of the time, but was not able to speak. She would have preferred it so, not being one to make farewell speeches. At eleven in the evening, very peacefully, with her nuns about her, she went to heaven. Thirteen hundred and sixty-eight of her religious were waiting to welcome her there. She had been fond of quoting St. Teresa's: "Lord Jesus, it is high time we saw each other!" There is every reason to believe He was as eager for the meeting as she.

They took her to Conflans, where she rested until France drove out her nuns, and then her body was removed to Jette, in Belgium, where in a shrine under the altar you may see still the strong, peaceful face Philippine Duchesne saw that first dull day in Grenoble. The Church confirmed her daughters' conviction of her holiness in 1908 when she was beatified, and in 1925 added the seal of canonization. Philippine Duchesne had died thirteen years before her, but with characteristic deference waited until 1940 before she was declared Blessed. Wars and persecutions have gone on ravaging Europe ever since Mother Barat died; but wars and persecutions were, she thought, the Society's native air. She had once said that Father de Tournély conceived the plan for the Society while he was being driven from city to city by the Revolution. What else should it expect? And God hates the peace of those He has destined for war. Nothing, she underlined again and again, nothing whatever happens unless God has planned it. And what He plans, He plans through love for our happiness. Therefore, trust Him, love Him, and let Him work through you.

Conclusion

Saints, we said, are consistent. In what had she been consistent? She was a woman with a great power of love and a great desire for happiness. As a child, she had realized that no happiness was either undiluted or lasting, and that no one was able to bear the whole weight of love she wanted to give. Deliberately, without any emotional fuss or blind groping, she decided she would give her love to God and find her happiness in Him. Nothing ever turned her from this decision, but she had too clear-sighted an understanding of her own limitations to think she could guide herself. The uncertain years when her brother was in prison taught her to believe God would work His Will in her if she would accept the will of those He put over her. She did, always, and though she might be terrified, she never allowed herself to be put off by what they asked. What was asked was that she teach others how to find happiness, and she taught them, of course, the same way she had found satisfying.

She brought up several generations of nuns on the principles of loving and giving and trusting God for the outcome. He was working out a design of love, and therefore devotion to the Sacred Heart, the source and symbol of Divine Love made human, was her obvious attraction. It was all she preached, by word and by example. Divine Love made human had encountered the obstacle of human sin, and the Cross was His way over that obstacle. The sufferings of Madeleine Sophie Barat's life, and the sufferings she taught her nuns and her children to accept, were to be a share in the Cross of Christ, a ransom for those who loved less, but who by the generosity of others might escape the effects of sin and come to love in spite of it.

Once, when she was a child, she had a favorite lamb, which clung to her all the time. Her brother told her that the lamb, by crouching silently but contentedly beside her, was loving her. She took the lamb as her model, and she clung to God. He did not allow her to be silent, and He arranged matters so that she had to struggle to be with Him as much as she wished, and so could not settle down contentedly. Like Mother d'Avenas, to whom she had written that it is doubly meritorious to be a sheep when one has not been born so, she was not a lamb by nature. But she made herself a lamb, just as Christ, Who could have been the Lion of Juda, made Himself the Lamb of God. She never refused anything she knew God wanted. Death was, therefore, for her, the finding of what she had been looking for through her long life: happiness in love, complete happiness in the love of God. That is why—in a time when love so often seems a farce or a risk and happiness a mirage—she is so excellent a model.